The Startup VC Guide

Everything Entrepreneurs Need to Know about Venture Capital and Startup Fundraising

Julian Ashford

ISBN: 9781807650490

Published by TPSA Publishing

Table of Contents

INTRODUCTION 9

Venture capital 11

What is Venture capital 15

Core activities of venture capitalists 15

How venture capitalists evaluate opportunities 16

Portfolio strategy and risk mitigation 17

Private equity investing and the meaning of the term 18

What is a venture capitalist 18

Investment focus and stages of investing 19

Length of investment and liquidity expectations 20

Corporate venturing 20

Commitments and fund raising 21

Capital calls 21

Illiquidity and long term commitment 21

Other types of funds and secondary partnerships 22

Advisors, gatekeepers, and fund of funds 22

Disbursements and financing rounds 22

Exits and how returns are realized 23

Initial public offering 23

Mergers and acquisitions 23

Valuations inside venture funds 23

Management fees 24

Carried interest 24

Venture Capital Firms and How They Operate 25

Active Participation and Value Creation 25

Stages of Investment Across the Business Life Cycle 25

Organizational Structure of Venture Capital Firms 26

How Venture Firms Create Synergies and Joint Support 27

Illiquidity and Why Venture Firms Cannot Exit Early 27

Sector Focus and Specialized Strategies 28

Common Features of Venture Capital Arrangements 28

Funding Sources and Capital Structure Considerations 29

Factors Influencing Capital Structure 29

Types of Venture Capital Firms 30

Organizational Forms and Fund Mechanics 30

Finding a Venture Capital Firm - The Six Key Variables to Consider 33

Location 33

Sector Preference 34

Stage Preference 34

Partners 35

Portfolio 35

Assets 35

Building a Target List and Approaching Firms Strategically 36

Consequences of Good Fit and Poor Fit 36

Obtaining Venture Capital For Business Startup 39

Different Forms of Venture Capital Money 39

Angel Investors as an Entry Point 40

Media and the Public Image of Venture Funding 41

Why Funding Can Be Harder After Market Booms 41

What Increases Your Chances of Getting Venture Capital 42

Preparing for the Process of Approaching Investors 42

A Realistic Conclusion 43

Venture Capital Financing Tips 45

What Venture Capital Really Is 45

How Venture Capital Differs from Bank Financing 45

Why IPOs and Acquisitions Matter 46

Negotiating Ownership and Terms Before Funding 46

The Main Disadvantage and Why Deals Fail 48

Founder Readiness and What Investors Expect 48
Fit Between Entrepreneur and Venture Firm 49
Choosing a Source of Venture Capital 49
Final Tips for Founders Seeking Venture Capital 50
Attracting Venture Capital 51
Understanding the Investor Mindset 51
Preparation as the Foundation 51
Building a Strong Business Plan and Executive Summary 52
Knowing the Funding Process of Each Investor 52
Clarity on Use of Capital 53
Creating a Target List and Running a Process 53
Preparing for the Meeting and the Questions 54
Practical Steps That Improve Attractiveness 54
Four Steps Towards Attracting Venture Capital Investments 55
Why Venture Capital Interest Keeps Growing 55
What Venture Capital Enables You to Do 55
Step One Networking and Building Real Relationships 56
Step Two Building an Experienced Team and Proving Execution Capacity 57
Step Three Creating a Professional Presentation That Answers Investor Questions 57
Step Four Using Media Coverage to Increase Credibility and Attention58
How the Four Steps Work Together 58
Final Guidance for Founders 59
How To Raise Venture Capital 61
Why Every Venture Capitalist Is Different 61
Two Common Investor Styles Herd Investors and Contrarian Investors61
Why Many Firms Avoid Duplicate Investments in the Same Subcategory 62
Why Venture Funds Need Big Outcomes 62
The Reality of Funding Challenges 63

Five Guidelines for Funding Through Venture Capitalists 63
Guideline Two Know the Investors and Choose the Right Type 64
Guideline Three Back to the Basics Keep the Pitch Clear and Tangible64
Guideline Four Do Not Depend on One Investor Create Options 65
Guideline Five Maintain the Relationship After Funding 65
Final Perspective 66
Elements of a Term-Sheet 67
Basics of the Offer 67
Closing date 67
Investors 67
Amount raised 68
Price per share 68
Pre money valuation 68
Capitalization 68
Basics of the Terms 68
Dividends and the type of preferred stock 69
Liquidation preference 69
Liquidation preference example and why it matters 69
Voting rights 70
Protective provisions 70
Anti dilution provisions 70
Redemption rights 71
Representations and warranties 71
Conditions to closing 71
Additional Terms in More Extensive Term Sheets 71
Information rights 71
Participation rights in future rounds 71
Registration rights 72
Investor approval requirements 72
Non disclosure and non compete provisions 72

Expiration date and no shop provision 72
Negotiation Priorities Valuation Versus Control 72
Main Reasons Companies Are Rejected by Venture Capital Funds 73
Deal size is too small 73
New company with very early stage risk 73
Lack of existing revenue or lack of traction proof 74
Too technical and difficult to understand 74
Relying too much on corporate advisors and brokers 75
Failing to show that you do not need the money to survive 75
The Core Principle Build First, Then Raise 75
Assets Are Not Only Financial 76
How to Use Rejection Constructively 76
Disclaimer 77
CONCLUSION 79

INTRODUCTION

This book exists to make those rules clear.

Most first time founders approach fundraising with an intuitive mindset. They assume that a great idea should naturally attract money. They focus on crafting a long business plan, polishing an elevator pitch, and sending messages to as many investors as possible. Then the rejections arrive, often fast and without explanation. The founder feels confused. The business is still fragile. Time is limited. And the entire process begins to look random, unfair, or impossible.

In reality, venture capital is not random. It is a system. Investors operate under mandates. They have preferred stages, preferred sectors, preferred geographies, and minimum check sizes. They make decisions based on risk, upside, timing, and the ability to exit. They look for traction and proof more than dreams and enthusiasm. They evaluate founders not only for brilliance, but for execution, clarity, and discipline. And they structure deals with term sheets designed to protect their capital while leaving room for extraordinary returns.

Once you understand this system, your perspective changes. Fundraising stops being a vague hunt for approval and becomes a strategic process. You begin to target the right investors instead of everyone. You learn what information matters and what does not. You prepare your company so that it fits the pattern investors recognize as investable. You avoid common mistakes that quietly destroy deals, from unclear positioning to messy financials to overly technical pitches. And when you finally reach the term sheet stage, you know what you are signing and what you must negotiate, not only to raise money, but to keep control of your company's future.

This book is written for inventors, entrepreneurs, and startup teams who want a practical guide to venture capital, from the first question of whether you should raise at all, to the final question of how you exit successfully. It explains what venture capital is, where it came from, why it matters, and how it differs from bank financing and other funding sources. It shows how venture firms operate, how they reduce risk through portfolios, and why they focus on big outcomes. It breaks down how to find the right venture capital firm by analyzing location, sector preference, stage preference, partners, portfolio fit, and assets. It also explores alternative paths such as angel investors, corporate venturing, and other funding structures that may be more realistic at certain stages.

Along the way, you will learn how investors actually think when they evaluate your company. You will see why some founders get meetings quickly while others are ignored. You will understand the role of networking, credibility, traction, and media signals. You will discover why preparation matters more than persuasion, and why a founder's ability to communicate simply can be more valuable than a founder's ability to impress with complexity.

A major part of this book is dedicated to the deal itself. Many entrepreneurs treat the term sheet as a formality, something that comes after the hard part. In truth, the term sheet is where the hard part becomes real. It is where valuation meets control, where founder optimism meets investor protection, and where the future of your ownership can be reshaped by clauses most founders do not fully understand. We will explore the elements of a term sheet, including pre money valuation, capitalization, dividends, liquidation preferences, voting rights, protective provisions, anti dilution provisions, redemption rights, representations and warranties, and conditions to closing. These topics can feel intimidating, but the goal here is not to turn you into a lawyer. The goal is to help you recognize what each term means in practice, why it is included, and how to negotiate what truly matters.

Finally, this book addresses the part of venture capital that no one likes to talk about but everyone experiences. Rejection. Venture capital funds reject most companies. Sometimes the deal is too small. Sometimes the company is too early. Sometimes there is no revenue or traction. Sometimes the pitch is too technical to understand. Sometimes founders rely too heavily on advisors instead of leading the process themselves. And sometimes the company looks like it needs money to survive rather than money to scale. Rejection is painful, but it is also information. Once you know the most common rejecting reasons, you can correct course and improve your odds the next time you walk into the room.

If you are reading this book, you do not need motivation. You need clarity. You need a map. You need a way to avoid wasting months chasing the wrong investors, telling the wrong story, or accepting the wrong terms. Venture capital is not meant for every business, and it is not meant for every founder. But if your company has the potential to scale, if your ambition is large, and if you are ready to grow into the demands of this kind of financing, then learning how venture capital works can be one of the most valuable business skills you ever develop.

The pages ahead will not promise shortcuts. They will not pretend fundraising is easy. Instead, they will give you the understanding to approach venture capital with strategy rather than hope, preparation rather than improvisation, and negotiation rather than surrender.

Let us begin with the foundation: what venture capital really is, why it exists, and how it became one of the most powerful engines of startup growth in the modern economy.

VENTURE CAPITAL

Venture capital is a form of financing in which investors commit money to a venture that is typically high risk, high uncertainty, and often unproven, usually in exchange for an equity stake and the possibility of outsized returns. The logic is straightforward. Many early stage ventures will fail or deliver only modest results, but a small number may grow rapidly and generate returns large enough to offset losses and still produce an attractive overall performance for investors. In this sense, venture capital is not simply risky investing. It is a structured approach to risk, built on the assumption that innovation often produces winner take most outcomes.

Although the idea of backing bold undertakings is as old as commerce itself, for example merchants financing voyages, patrons supporting inventors, and industrialists funding new machinery, the modern practice of venture capitalism remained scattered for much of history. Wealthy individuals, families, and small partnerships sometimes supported entrepreneurs, but there was little standardization in how such deals were sourced, evaluated, governed, and exited. Only in the last several decades has venture capital evolved into a recognizable industry with common institutional structures, specialized firms, repeatable methods, and a mature ecosystem of legal, financial, and professional services. This coalescence occurred most visibly in the United States, where a unique combination of research universities, government policy, deep capital markets, and entrepreneurial culture provided a fertile environment.

The origins of venture capital in its modern form are often traced to General Georges Doriot, a professor at Harvard Business School who helped formalize the approach after World War Two. In 1946, he established American Research and Development, an organization designed to finance the commercial exploitation of technologies emerging from United States universities and research laboratories. The premise was forward looking. Scientific advances were accelerating, but transforming research into products required capital, managerial discipline, and patience, three things that young companies usually lack. American Research and Development and similar initiatives helped demonstrate that professional investors could systematically fund innovation, guide management, and eventually realize gains through public listings or acquisitions.

Public policy also played a meaningful role. In the United States, legislative and regulatory changes, including frameworks enabling the licensing and support of Small Business Investment Companies through the Small Business Administration, helped channel capital into smaller, growth oriented firms. This created an environment where institutional money could be deployed into ventures that were too small, too young, or too uncertain to qualify for traditional bank loans. Unlike banks, which rely on collateral and predictable cash flows, venture capitalists rely on future value creation. They accept that near term profits may be nonexistent because the company is investing in product development, market entry, and scale.

As the model proved itself, large corporations began entering the space through corporate venture capital arms. Companies like Xerox, 3M, and General Electric pursued strategic investments to stay close to emerging technologies, new business models, and disruptive competitors. Corporate venture investing provided not only funding but also industry expertise, distribution networks, and credibility for young firms, while giving large corporations an option on future innovation. These developments in the United States influenced other regions, helping venture capital spread globally, though adoption rates differed based on local markets, regulation, and cultural attitudes toward risk and failure.

Early attempts to establish venture capital ecosystems in many countries during the 1970s were often limited or uneven. Capital markets were smaller, entrepreneurial pipelines were thinner, and legal structures for equity participation and exits were less developed. But the economic and technological shifts of the 1980s, particularly the rapid rise of high technology industries, created new demand for growth finance. Personal computing, semiconductors, biotechnology, and later the internet economy demonstrated that small teams could build products with global reach. As these industries expanded, venture capital grew quickly. The opportunity set widened, exits became more feasible, and a supporting ecosystem of accelerators, specialized law firms, investment banks, and talent networks began to mature.

In practice, venture capital plays its most visible role in financing startups and early stage businesses, as well as companies in turnaround situations where a business needs capital and expertise to pivot, restructure, or reignite growth. Venture capital differs from simple funding because it is typically active capital. Venture firms frequently take board seats, influence major strategic decisions, help recruit executives, introduce customers or partners, and shape the company's path toward the next stage, whether that is a larger funding round, an acquisition, or an initial public offering. This involvement is partly protective, ensuring governance and discipline, and partly value adding, increasing the odds of success.

A typical venture capital firm raises money from multiple sources, often called limited partners, such as pension funds, university endowments, insurance companies, sovereign wealth funds, family offices, and high net worth individuals. The venture firm, acting as the general partner, manages the fund and makes investment decisions according to a defined strategy, including sector focus, geography, stage, and target ownership. The fund usually has a finite life, often around ten years, and returns are realized through exits, most commonly acquisitions or public listings. Because profits depend heavily on timing and market cycles, venture capital is shaped by broader economic conditions, interest rates, and the health of public markets.

To understand where venture capital fits inside a business, it helps to distinguish the types of funds a company may use. Some capital, like share capital or equity, is permanent in the sense that it does not have a fixed repayment date. Equity investors are compensated through ownership, dividends are rare in high growth startups, and appreciation in the company's value. Other funds, like debentures or long term loans, stay in the business for extended periods and involve contractual repayment obligations, usually with interest. Short term funds, like trade credit, short term borrowings, or working capital lines, support daily operations and may fluctuate frequently with sales cycles and cash needs.

The overall mix of these financing sources is known as the firm's financial structure. When analysts speak more narrowly about long term financing choices, primarily the blend of equity and long term debt, they refer to the capital structure. Venture capital usually enters the capital structure on the equity side, or via equity like instruments such as convertible preferred shares. This is significant. Equity financing does not burden a young company with fixed interest payments, which can be fatal when revenues are uncertain. However, it does dilute ownership. Founders give up a portion of the company and often some control. This trade off is central to venture backed growth. Founders exchange a slice of upside for the capital, expertise, and momentum needed to build something much larger.

In the end, venture capital is best understood as a specialized bridge between invention and scale. It finances uncertainty, accelerates innovation, and helps transform new technologies and bold ideas into functioning companies. Its history shows a gradual shift from fragmented individual patronage to an institutional professional system, one that thrives when markets reward growth, when research and entrepreneurship are strong, and when pathways to exit exist. For businesses, venture capital is not just money, but a strategic component of capital structure, designed to absorb risk in the present in pursuit of extraordinary value in the future.

WHAT IS VENTURE CAPITAL

Venture capital is money provided by professional investors who invest alongside a company's management in young, rapidly growing businesses that have the potential to become significant contributors to the economy. In practical terms, it is one of the most important sources of equity financing for startups and early stage companies, especially those that are building new products, entering new markets, or commercializing new technologies. What makes venture capital different from many other forms of financing is the combination of risk, active involvement, and patience. Venture investors accept that uncertainty is high, that profits may be delayed, and that many investments may not succeed, because the few that do succeed can grow so dramatically that they drive the overall returns of the fund.

Venture capital is usually delivered through professionally managed venture firms that are organized as private partnerships or closely held corporations. These firms manage capital raised from a wide range of investors. Common sources include public and private pension funds, university endowments, charitable foundations, corporations, wealthy individuals, foreign investors, and the venture capitalists themselves. The reason so many institutional investors participate is that venture capital can offer diversification and the possibility of higher long term returns, even though it also involves longer holding periods and limited liquidity.

In most cases, the venture firm forms a fund, raises commitments from investors, and then invests that money into a portfolio of companies over a period of years. The fund structure exists because venture investing works best when risk is spread across many bets, rather than concentrated in a single company. A single fund might invest in ten, twenty, or more companies, knowing that outcomes will vary widely. Some may fail, some may break even, and a small number may become very valuable.

Core activities of venture capitalists

Venture capitalists are not simply people who write checks. Their role combines capital allocation, strategic judgment, and active support. Their work can be understood through several core activities.

First, they finance new and rapidly growing companies. These companies often cannot obtain bank loans because they lack stable cash flow and sufficient collateral. Venture capital fills this gap by providing equity capital that does not require monthly repayments.

Second, they purchase equity securities or equity like instruments. While the specifics differ from deal to deal, venture financing usually results in ownership for the investors. This aligns incentives because investors benefit when the company's value increases.

Third, they assist in the development of new products or services. This assistance may be direct, through advice and introductions, or indirect, through setting performance milestones and building accountability into the governance of the company.

Fourth, they add value through active participation. This is one of the defining features of venture capital. Many venture firms take a board seat, help recruit senior leadership, refine business strategy, and strengthen go to market execution. They may also help a company professionalize its reporting, budgeting, hiring, and legal foundations.

Fifth, they accept higher risk in exchange for the possibility of higher reward. Venture investments are typically made in markets where outcomes are uncertain, competition evolves quickly, and technology or consumer behavior can shift. The aim is to find companies that, if successful, can grow by orders of magnitude.

Sixth, they operate with a long term orientation. Venture investors typically expect that it will take years for a company to mature. They plan for multiple funding rounds, product iterations, market learning, and scaling phases.

How venture capitalists evaluate opportunities

When considering an investment, venture capitalists screen both technical and business fundamentals. They review far more companies than they fund, often looking at hundreds of opportunities to select only a few. This selectivity is not simply caution. It is a recognition that venture outcomes are highly skewed, and only a small fraction of companies will have the combination of market size, product advantage, execution capability, and timing that supports major growth.

A typical evaluation includes several dimensions.

Market. Venture firms look for large and expanding markets, or markets that can be reshaped by a new approach. A strong company in a small market may still struggle to produce venture scale returns.

Product and differentiation. Investors ask what is unique, why it matters, and how defensible it is. Defensibility can come from technology, data, distribution advantages, partnerships, regulation, brand, or network effects.

Team. Because early stage companies change constantly, the capabilities of founders and management are critical. Investors assess leadership, resilience, learning speed, and the ability to recruit talent.

Business model. The company must have a plausible path to sustainable economics. That includes pricing power, customer acquisition dynamics, retention, unit economics, and scalability.

Execution plan and milestones. Venture investors often structure financing around milestones. They want clarity on how capital will be used, what results should follow, and what risks remain.

After investing, venture capitalists typically work closely with management to improve execution. They contribute experience gained from working with other companies facing similar growth challenges, such as scaling operations, entering new markets, managing rapid hiring, building sales teams, and navigating competitive threats.

Portfolio strategy and risk mitigation

Because venture investing involves significant uncertainty, venture capitalists mitigate risk by building a portfolio of young companies within a single fund. The idea is not that every investment must succeed. Rather, the portfolio is constructed so that a few strong successes can compensate for weaker outcomes. This is why venture investors care so much about potential upside. When a company succeeds in a major way, it can return a large multiple of the original investment.

Co investment is also common. Multiple venture firms may invest together in a company, a practice often called syndication. Syndication can bring several benefits. It can increase the total capital available to the company, combine expertise from different investors, expand networks and introductions, and share risk among firms.

Many venture partnerships manage multiple funds simultaneously. They may have one fund focused on early stage investments and another on later stage opportunities. Managing multiple funds also allows the firm to continue supporting successful companies in later rounds, which can be important because the best companies often need more capital as they scale.

Over decades, venture capital has supported the growth of many technology and entrepreneurial communities. It has contributed to job creation, innovation, and competitiveness by accelerating the development of new industries and companies. Well known examples of companies that received venture funding early include Apple, Intel, Microsoft, and Genentech, among many others. These examples illustrate how venture capital can provide the resources and guidance needed for young companies to grow into global leaders.

Private equity investing and the meaning of the term

Venture capital investing grew from a relatively small pool of capital in the 1960s and early 1970s into a mainstream asset class that is now a significant part of many institutional portfolios. Over time, some investors began using the term private equity investing to refer broadly to both venture investing and buyout investing. This can create confusion because in some contexts the term private equity is used narrowly to refer only to buyout funds that acquire established businesses, often using significant debt.

It helps to distinguish the two.

Venture capital typically invests in young companies that are still developing products and markets. Risk is higher, profitability is often far away, and success depends on growth and market creation.

Buyout investing typically targets mature businesses with stable cash flows. The investor often acquires control and focuses on operational improvements, strategic repositioning, and financial restructuring. Debt may be used to enhance returns.

In institutional asset allocation, venture capital and buyout funds are often grouped under the broader category of alternative assets. Many institutions allocate a small percentage of their portfolio, such as two percent to three percent, to alternatives like venture capital and buyouts, depending on their risk tolerance and liquidity needs. A significant portion of venture and private equity capital has traditionally come from public and private pension funds, with the remainder coming from endowments, foundations, insurance companies, banks, individuals, and other entities seeking diversification and higher expected returns.

What is a venture capitalist

Many people imagine a venture capitalist as a wealthy financier who funds startups. The popular story goes like this. A founder has a powerful invention or a world changing idea, needs money, cannot get a bank loan, and therefore turns to a venture capitalist.

There is some truth in this story, but it misses important details. Venture capitalists are usually part of a firm that manages pooled capital raised from many investors. That firm is often organized as a limited partnership, where the general partner makes investment decisions and the limited partners provide most of the capital. The venture capitalist's job is to deploy that capital into companies with the potential to produce a high rate of return within a period often measured in years, commonly five to seven, though this can vary.

A venture capitalist also differs from a passive investor because they often play an active role in company building. They may help with management decisions, strategy, positioning, recruiting, partnerships, fundraising, and preparing for an eventual exit. Many venture capitalists see themselves as entrepreneurs first and financiers second, because they spend much of their time solving business problems rather than simply analyzing spreadsheets.

Individuals can also be venture investors. In earlier decades, individual investors were archetypal venture financiers. While institutional venture firms became dominant over time, individuals have again become influential through angel investing. Angel investors often invest early, provide mentoring, and contribute expertise. Some angels are experienced executives, retired business leaders, or founders who have built companies before. Their value is often in their guidance and network, not only their capital.

Investment focus and stages of investing

Venture capitalists can be generalists or specialists depending on strategy. Generalist investors may invest across many industries, geographic regions, and stages of a company's life. Specialist investors may focus on one sector, such as software, healthcare, or energy, or on a specific region, or on a specific stage, such as seed stage.

Not all venture capital is strictly about startups. Venture firms invest across a range of stages.

Seed investing refers to investing before there is a fully developed product or even a fully formed company. The goal is to support initial product exploration, early hiring, and proof of concept. Risk is high because much remains unknown.

Early stage investing typically supports companies that have formed a business, built an early product, and are testing the market. Funding is used to refine the product, find product market fit, build early sales or distribution, and establish repeatable growth.

Expansion stage financing supports a company that has found traction and needs capital to scale. This may include building larger teams, entering new markets, expanding production, improving infrastructure, and strengthening customer support. The company may still be unprofitable, but the core model shows signs of scalability.

Later stage investing can support a company approaching a public offering or preparing for a major acquisition. The focus often shifts toward governance, predictable performance, risk management, and financial discipline, because public markets and large acquirers demand stability and clarity.

Some funds also specialize in acquisition, turnaround, or recapitalization situations. In these cases, the company may be underperforming, mismanaged, or facing financial distress, and the investor sees an opportunity to restore value through restructuring and strategic change.

Venture funds can be broadly diversified across industries, or narrowly focused on a particular technology or market. While technology investing has historically received much attention in the United States, venture capital also supports sectors such as industrial products, construction related services, business services, retail, and companies pursuing socially responsible missions.

Across all these approaches, a common denominator remains. The venture capitalist is not a passive investor. They typically have an active and vested interest in guiding and growing the companies they back, drawing on patterns learned from investing in many companies over time. Some venture firms also create synergies within their portfolio, connecting companies that can help each other, such as pairing a company with a strong product with another company that has stronger distribution or sales capabilities.

Length of investment and liquidity expectations

Venture capitalists help companies grow, but they eventually seek to exit their investments, often within three to seven years of the initial investment. The exact timeline depends on the stage of the investment and the speed of company development. An early stage investment can take seven to ten years to mature, while a later stage investment may reach liquidity in fewer years.

This matters because venture investing is not liquid in the way public stocks are liquid. Limited partners commit capital for a long period and must plan their liquidity needs accordingly. Venture funds are designed with this long duration in mind. The investment must be made with careful diligence and expertise because there is no simple way to sell the position quickly.

Corporate venturing

Corporate venturing, sometimes called direct investing, involves investments made by venture programs or subsidiaries of nonfinancial corporations. These programs became especially visible in the 1980s and have regained popularity in many periods since. The corporate investor seeks opportunities that align with the parent company's strategy, technology roadmap, or competitive needs. The goal may be synergy, access to innovation, new product channels, or cost savings, not just financial return.

Corporate venturing programs can be loosely connected to business development teams, or they can be structured as more independent entities with a defined mission and strategic charter. Some venture firms also specialize in advising and managing corporate venturing programs.

A useful distinction is that corporate venturing often prioritizes strategic objectives, while traditional venture funds prioritize investment returns. In reality, both considerations can exist in both models. Still, the emphasis can differ. Another distinction is the source of capital. Corporate programs usually invest the corporation's own capital, while traditional venture funds invest capital committed by external limited partners.

Commitments and fund raising

The process venture firms use to obtain investment commitments from investors is typically called fund raising. This should not be confused with the process of raising capital for a startup, which is also sometimes called fund raising. In a venture fund context, fund raising refers to building the fund itself.

A venture firm sets a target fund size, presents its strategy and track record to potential investors, and distributes offering documents describing terms and risks. The process can take weeks or months. Commitments are made during the formation period, and once sufficient commitments are secured, the firm begins investing.

Because of the risk, the long holding period, and the illiquidity, and because minimum commitments can be large, venture fund investing has traditionally been out of reach for many individuals. Funds may have a small number of limited partners or close to one hundred, depending on fund size and investor type.

Capital calls

When the venture firm begins making investments, it does not usually collect all committed capital immediately. Instead, it calls capital from limited partners as needed. These are called capital calls. The capital is collected in tranches over time, sometimes referred to as paid in capital.

In earlier periods, firms might have called capital in a more predictable pattern over a multi year period. More recently, many firms synchronize capital calls with investment needs, drawing capital as required for deals and follow on investments. This approach can be more efficient for investors because it reduces idle cash and aligns contributions with actual deployment.

Illiquidity and long term commitment

Limited partners invest in venture funds knowing that capital will be tied up for a long time. It may take several years before early investments produce proceeds, and in many cases capital can remain invested for seven to ten years. This illiquidity is not a minor detail. It is central to the decision to invest in venture funds and must be considered in portfolio planning. Institutions that invest in venture capital typically have long time horizons, allowing them to accept illiquidity in exchange for potentially higher returns.

Other types of funds and secondary partnerships

Because venture funds are private partnerships, there is typically no simple way to exit before the fund matures or expires. However, secondary markets have developed. Secondary partnerships specialize in purchasing portfolios of investments from existing venture investors. This can provide liquidity to original investors, who may want to rebalance or free up capital earlier than expected. Secondary investors often look for undervalued or mispriced assets and seek strong returns by buying at a discount relative to perceived future value.

Advisors, gatekeepers, and fund of funds

Choosing which venture funds to invest in is similar to selecting a skilled manager, but the decision is more complex because the commitment is long term and performance data can be difficult to interpret. Larger institutions may invest in many funds and continue committing to new funds each year.

Some limited partners lack the resources or expertise to evaluate many funds, so they delegate the process to investment advisors, sometimes called gatekeepers. These advisors pool assets from multiple clients and invest as limited partners in venture or buyout funds.

Another approach is a fund of funds. A fund of funds is a partnership designed to invest in multiple other funds. This can provide diversification and allow investors to commit smaller amounts across a broader set of managers, though it can also add an additional layer of fees.

Disbursements and financing rounds

Investments made by venture funds into portfolio companies are often called disbursements. Companies usually receive capital in one or more rounds of financing, depending on growth needs and milestone achievement. A venture firm may invest alone, but more often invests alongside others through syndication.

Syndication can strengthen the company by increasing available capital and bringing complementary expertise. Each investor may contribute different advantages, such as sector knowledge, recruiting networks, customer introductions, operational guidance, or later stage funding capacity.

A venture firm often takes a board seat to support governance and increase the likelihood of success. The firm may also reserve a portion of its fund to support follow on rounds in its strongest companies. This reserve strategy matters because successful companies often require additional capital to scale, and maintaining ownership in winners can be a major driver of returns.

Exits and how returns are realized

A venture firm typically seeks to exit an investment within a period aligned with its fund strategy, often three to five years for some strategies, and longer for others. While an initial public offering is a highly visible type of exit, many successful exits occur through mergers and acquisitions. In any exit, the venture firm's experience in structuring and timing the transaction can influence the ultimate result for both the fund and the founders.

Initial public offering

An initial public offering is one of the most visible exits. When a venture backed company goes public, the venture firm is usually treated as an insider. It receives public shares but may face restrictions on how and when those shares can be sold. After lockup periods and other restrictions end, the fund can distribute shares or cash proceeds to limited partners. Limited partners can then hold or sell the public shares as part of their own portfolio management.

Mergers and acquisitions

Mergers and acquisitions are the most common form of successful venture exit. In an acquisition, the acquiring company pays cash, stock, or a combination. The venture firm distributes proceeds to limited partners according to fund terms. Acquisitions can occur at many stages, including before an initial public offering is feasible, and may be driven by strategic fit, technology acquisition, market expansion, or competitive consolidation.

Valuations inside venture funds

Like other investment vehicles, each venture fund has a net asset value that represents the estimated value of investor holdings at a given time. Unlike a mutual fund, however, this value is not usually determined by daily public market transactions. Instead, it is based on valuations of private portfolio companies, plus any public holdings held by the fund.

Private company valuation is typically based on financing rounds, comparable company analysis, revenue multiples, discounted cash flow assumptions, or other accepted methods. In many cases, a company's valuation is anchored to the price paid in the most recent financing round. Between rounds, valuations may remain stable unless a material event occurs, such as a major revenue change, a new financing, an acquisition offer, a write down due to poor performance, or a significant market shift.

If the fund holds shares in public companies that are still subject to restrictions, those holdings may be discounted for liquidity in fund reporting. Valuation practices tend to be conservative, particularly for early stage funds, because uncertainty is higher and the time to exit is longer.

Management fees

The general partner of a venture fund typically charges a management fee to cover the costs of managing the fund. This pays for salaries, sourcing, due diligence, legal and administrative costs, portfolio support, and operations. Management fees are usually paid regularly over the life of the fund and may decline in later years as the fund shifts from investing to managing and exiting its portfolio.

Carried interest

Carried interest refers to the share of profits allocated to the general partner as compensation for managing the fund and producing returns. It is effectively the performance based component of venture fund economics. The size and calculation of carried interest can vary widely by fund and by negotiated terms. Some funds include hurdles, preferred returns, or other mechanisms that shape when and how carry is earned. Regardless of structure, carried interest is designed to align incentives by rewarding the general partner when investors achieve strong results.

VENTURE CAPITAL FIRMS AND HOW THEY OPERATE

Venture capital firms operate with long term plans. Their approach is built on the idea that real company building takes time and that the biggest value is created over multiple years, not in a short cycle. Because of this long horizon, venture capital firms are often willing to take higher risks than traditional lenders or conservative investors. They accept uncertainty about technology, market adoption, competitors, and execution because they invest with the intention of earning higher rewards if the company succeeds.

This willingness to take risk is not random or impulsive. It is usually disciplined and structured. Venture firms understand that many early stage companies will not become large successes. Some will fail completely, while others may survive but never scale. Venture firms therefore focus on opportunities where the potential upside is very large, because the success of a few investments can compensate for weaker outcomes across the rest of the portfolio. The risk is high, but the expected payoff is designed to be high as well.

Active Participation and Value Creation

Venture capitalists are not only passive financiers. They are often deeply involved in the companies they support. Their participation can include helping founders refine strategy, validating the market approach, strengthening the leadership team, and improving the company's ability to execute. In many cases, the venture investor becomes a partner in company building, not only a provider of capital.

This active participation tends to concentrate in three areas: management, strategic marketing, and planning. On the management side, venture capitalists may support recruiting key executives, structuring incentives, setting governance processes, and improving operational discipline. On the strategic marketing side, they may help define target customers, clarify positioning, refine pricing strategy, and improve the go to market plan. On the planning side, they often support milestone setting, budgeting, resource allocation, and long term roadmaps.

Because of this hands on involvement, venture capitalists are often described as entrepreneurs first and financiers second. They work with teams to solve real business problems. They apply lessons learned from prior investments, share patterns, and help companies avoid common growth mistakes. The best venture capitalists function like experienced advisors who know how fast growing companies break, how they recover, and how they scale.

Stages of Investment Across the Business Life Cycle

It is true that venture firms commonly invest in companies in their early stages of growth, but venture capital is not limited to only the earliest moments of a company's life. Many venture capitalists invest across multiple stages of the business life cycle, depending on their strategy.

Seed stage investing is the earliest point. This is where a venture capitalist may invest before the real product has been launched, sometimes even before a company is fully formed. At this stage, the investment is supporting exploration: building a prototype, testing the market, hiring early talent, and validating that the problem and solution truly fit.

Early stage investing usually comes when a product exists in some form and the company is testing customers or early traction. Venture capital at this stage is used to reach product market fit, which means proving that customers consistently want the product and are willing to pay for it. It is also used to build the first repeatable sales and marketing processes.

Expansion stage investing supports a company that has traction and wants to grow aggressively. The goal here is scale. Funding is used to expand operations, hire larger teams, invest in customer acquisition, enter new markets, strengthen product capabilities, and build infrastructure that can support growth. This can involve scaling production, expanding a software platform, building distribution, or increasing service capacity.

Later stage venture investing supports companies that are approaching major liquidity events or large strategic transitions. This can include preparing for a public offering, strengthening financial reporting and governance, or positioning the company for a major acquisition. The company at this stage may be much larger, with proven revenue, but still needs capital to grow and to become robust enough for public markets or large acquirers.

Organizational Structure of Venture Capital Firms

There are many types of venture capital firms and funds. One common structure is a limited partnership. In this arrangement, the venture capital firm serves as the general partner, meaning it manages the fund and makes investment decisions. The investors in the fund are limited partners, meaning they provide capital but typically do not control investment decisions.

The most common type of venture firm is the independent venture capital firm. It is not affiliated with other financial institutions. It operates as a private independent firm that raises capital from investors and invests based on its own strategy. This independence can be attractive because it allows the firm to focus primarily on investment performance and company growth, without conflicts tied to banking, insurance, or other institutional priorities.

Other types of venture firms include those affiliated with commercial banks, investment banks, or insurance companies. These firms may invest on behalf of outside investors, on behalf of clients, or in some cases as part of a broader financial services strategy.

Another category includes corporate venture investors. These are venture arms of nonfinancial corporations that invest the parent company's capital. Their goals often include strategic benefits such as access to new technologies, partnerships, innovation pipelines, and competitive intelligence, along with financial returns. Corporate venture investing can be especially valuable when the corporation can help portfolio companies with distribution, manufacturing, regulation, or customer access.

There are also government affiliated investment programs that support startups through state, local, or national initiatives. These programs are often designed to encourage innovation, job creation, and competitiveness, especially in sectors that are important for national development.

How Venture Firms Create Synergies and Joint Support

Some venture firms increase their effectiveness by creating collaboration and synergies among companies in their portfolio. When the portfolio is constructed thoughtfully, one company may help another through partnerships, shared customers, technology integration, or operational support.

A common example involves a company with a strong product but weak distribution. If another company, or another team in the broader venture network, has better distribution technology or sales capability, the venture firm may facilitate a connection. The goal is to reduce friction, accelerate growth, and help both companies become stronger. These relationships are not guaranteed, and they must be aligned with the interests of each company. When done well, however, portfolio synergy can become a competitive advantage for the venture firm and a growth lever for the startups.

Illiquidity and Why Venture Firms Cannot Exit Early

Venture firms are private investment entities and their investments are not easily sold at will. In most cases, they cannot fully exit an investment before it reaches maturity through a liquidity event. This is because the companies they invest in are private and their shares are not traded on public markets. The result is that venture investing is illiquid by nature.

This illiquidity shapes the behavior of the entire venture ecosystem. It forces long term planning, careful selection, and a focus on building sustainable value. It also influences the relationship between founders and investors. Both sides understand that value is realized primarily through exits such as acquisitions or public offerings, and those outcomes take time.

What Venture Capital Firms Look For and Who Venture Capital Is For
A venture capital firm can be understood as a private partnership that provides

opportunities for entrepreneurs to grow rapidly. Venture firms evaluate opportunities with caution and discipline because their capital is committed for long periods and because each investment decision affects the overall success of the fund. They are always attentive to the potential rate of return of each investment, not because they ignore mission or innovation, but because fund survival depends on generating strong outcomes.

Venture capital is not meant for everyone and it is not meant for every type of entrepreneur. It is best suited to entrepreneurs who aim to build large companies, enter big markets, and grow aggressively. Venture capital comes with expectations. It usually requires rapid scaling, ambitious targets, and a willingness to accept external influence in governance and strategic decisions. Entrepreneurs seeking slower, steady growth or full independence may find venture capital to be the wrong match.

Because of these expectations, venture capitalists review many investment opportunities before selecting only a few. The companies that receive funding are typically those that show favorable investment characteristics: large market potential, credible execution capability, a compelling product, and the possibility of strong competitive advantage.

Sector Focus and Specialized Strategies

Venture capitalists may invest across many sectors or specialize in a narrow set of industries. Some invest broadly and may support companies in construction, industrial products, business services, and other nontechnology sectors. Others follow specialized strategies. One investor may focus on retail companies, while another may prefer companies that are newly formed and need support at the earliest stage. Some may focus on healthcare, enterprise software, consumer products, climate technology, or financial services. Specialization can improve decision quality because deep sector knowledge helps investors evaluate risks and identify the most promising opportunities.

Specialization also affects how venture capitalists add value. A sector focused investor can provide more relevant introductions, sharper strategic advice, and better hiring support because they understand the specific dynamics of the industry.

Common Features of Venture Capital Arrangements

Even though the terms and conditions of venture capital are not fully standardized, there are several features that appear frequently.

High risk, high return expectation is central. Venture capital firms accept a high degree of risk in exchange for the expectation of earning a high rate of return if the company succeeds.

Active guidance is another common feature. Venture capital firms do not only provide funds. They take an active interest in guiding the company through strategy, governance, and operational development.

Limited financial burden in early years is also typical. Since venture capital is usually equity, the company is not required to make interest payments like it would with a loan. This reduces cash pressure in the earliest years when a company is still building product and customer base.

Planned liquidity timeline is important. Venture capital firms usually plan to liquidate their investment after a period that often ranges from three to five years, though it can be longer depending on stage and market conditions. They do not invest expecting permanent ownership. They invest expecting eventual exit through acquisition or public offering.

Founder options and repurchase possibilities may exist. In some arrangements, the promoter or founder may be given the first option to acquire the equity stake held by the venture capital firm, depending on terms and governance rules. This can matter in cases where founders want to regain ownership or consolidate control during later stages.

Funding Sources and Capital Structure Considerations

Venture capital firms can raise funds from many sources, and the companies they invest in can also build their own financing structures using different instruments. Long term financing sources for companies can include equity shares, preference shares, debentures of different types, term loans from financial institutions, and retained reserves generated from profits over time.

A firm can choose different combinations of these sources depending on cost, availability, and impact on company value and control. This creates different patterns of capital structure. Some companies rely only on equity shares. Others combine equity and preference shares. Others use a mix of equity and debentures, or equity plus preference shares plus reserves, and so on. Each combination changes the risk profile, the cost of capital, and the distribution of control and returns among stakeholders.

Factors Influencing Capital Structure

The capital structure of companies, including venture backed companies, is influenced by several factors. One important concept is trading on equity, which refers to using long term fixed interest financing alongside equity capital. If a company can earn a return on investment that is higher than the cost of the fixed interest financing, it can increase returns to equity holders. However, this approach also increases risk because fixed obligations must be paid regardless of performance. Many early stage venture backed startups avoid significant debt for this reason, choosing equity until cash flows become stable.

Other influencing factors include growth rate and stability of sales. Companies with predictable, stable revenues may have more flexibility to use debt safely. Companies with volatile or uncertain revenues often prefer equity, because it reduces the risk of financial distress during downturns.

Types of Venture Capital Firms

Several types of venture capital firms exist, but most mainstream firms invest through funds organized as limited partnerships in which the venture capital firm serves as the general partner.

Private independent firms are the most common. They have no affiliation with other financial institutions and invest based on their own strategy.

Affiliated venture firms are connected to banks or insurance companies. They may invest on behalf of clients or as part of a broader financial platform.

Corporate venture investors are subsidiaries of industrial corporations investing the parent's capital for strategic and financial aims.

Government affiliated programs support startups through public initiatives. One well known example historically has been the SBIC program administered by the Small Business Administration, through which venture firms could augment their own funds with government supported financing and leverage investments into qualified companies.

Organizational Forms and Fund Mechanics

While the limited partnership remains the predominant form of organization, tax and legal structures have also allowed alternatives such as limited liability partnerships and limited liability companies. Each form involves tradeoffs around liability, taxation, and management responsibilities. Even when alternative forms are used, the core logic stays similar: outside investors provide capital and the manager makes investment decisions under agreed terms.

The venture capital firm organizes its partnership as a pooled fund, meaning the fund includes the general partner and the limited partners. These funds are often fixed life partnerships, commonly with a life of around ten years. The fund is capitalized by commitments from limited partners. Once the fund reaches its target size, it is closed to further commitments so it has a fixed pool of capital from which to make investments. This fixed pool discipline encourages thoughtful allocation and ensures that the firm can focus on investing and supporting companies rather than constantly adjusting fund size.

A successful venture firm may manage more than one fund at a time. It may raise a new fund a few years after closing the first to continue investing and to provide opportunities for new and existing investors. It is not unusual for a strong firm to raise multiple funds over a decade or more. Each fund is managed separately, has its own investors, and typically has its own strategy, which may be similar to or different from other funds in the firm. One fund might focus on early stage deals, another on later stage growth, and another on a diversified approach, depending on the firm's overall strategy.

FINDING A VENTURE CAPITAL FIRM - THE SIX KEY VARIABLES TO CONSIDER

Many ventures face the difficult task of raising venture capital. The first and most important part of this process is finding the right venture capital firm. This step is often underestimated. At first glance, it may seem like funding is simply a matter of presenting a strong idea to any investor with money. In reality, venture capital works through fit. A company can be excellent and still be rejected if it does not match a firm's strategy, geographic focus, sector expertise, or stage preference. This is why many companies fail to raise the capital they need. They spend time pitching the wrong investors, receive predictable rejections, lose momentum, and sometimes run out of cash before they find the right match.

There are thousands of venture capital firms in the United States alone, and many more globally. They differ in what they invest in, how they invest, what level of involvement they provide, and what outcomes they pursue. A founder who understands these differences can approach fundraising strategically. Instead of trying to convince everyone, the founder focuses on the limited set of firms that are structurally able and willing to invest. This increases the probability of success and reduces wasted effort.

When seeking a venture capital firm, there are six key variables to consider: location, sector preference, stage preference, partners, portfolio, and assets. Each of these variables influences whether a firm will seriously evaluate your opportunity, how helpful they can be after investing, and whether they can continue supporting you over time.

Location

Location is often more important than founders expect. Many venture capital firms invest relatively close to their offices, sometimes within a limited radius. The reason is practical. Venture capitalists add value through involvement. They attend board meetings, support hiring, connect founders to networks, and respond quickly during difficult moments. Doing this is easier when the company is within reach. Even in an era of remote work, many investors still prefer proximity because it increases access, improves relationship quality, and makes collaboration smoother.

For a founder, this means geography shapes the investor list. If you are building a company in a specific city or region, you should prioritize firms that already invest there, have portfolio companies nearby, or openly state a willingness to invest across wider geographies. Some firms are truly global. Others have a strong local footprint and rarely invest far away. A well targeted search prevents you from wasting time on firms whose internal rules effectively block your deal from the start.

Sector Preference

Most venture capital firms have sector preferences. This means they focus on certain industries or categories such as healthcare, information technology, wireless technologies, biotechnology, consumer goods, financial technology, enterprise software, climate solutions, or other defined themes. Sector focus exists because expertise matters. Investors want to understand the market, evaluate competitive dynamics, judge the strength of the product, and provide helpful guidance. It is difficult to do this without familiarity.

For founders, sector preference is a filter. If your company is outside a firm's sector focus, you may be rejected even if your company is strong. This is not always a judgment on quality. It can simply mean the firm's mandate does not allow it, or the partners do not feel qualified to support you. The goal is not to convince a firm to change its identity. The goal is to find firms whose identity already matches your business.

Sector preference also affects the kind of value an investor can add. A sector aligned investor can provide better introductions to customers and partners, stronger hiring support, sharper strategic insights, and more credibility in the market. A misaligned investor may still be supportive, but will often be less effective because their network and experience are not tailored to your domain.

Stage Preference

Venture capital firms also differ by stage preference. Some specialize in early stage investing, where the company may have limited revenue and the product may still be evolving. These investors accept higher uncertainty because early entry can lead to larger ownership and higher potential returns if the company becomes successful. Early stage investors often help founders shape the business model, refine the product, and reach product market fit.

Other venture capital firms prefer later stages. They may invest when the company already has strong traction, growing revenue, and a clearer path to scale. Some focus on bridging companies toward public markets or providing capital for major expansion. These later stage investors tend to care more about measurable performance, scalability, and operational maturity, because the company is expected to move toward a liquidity event or a large acquisition.

A founder should match the fundraising stage to the investor's stage focus. Pitching a seed stage company to a firm that only invests at growth stage usually ends in rejection, even if the company is promising. Likewise, pitching a later stage company to a seed focused firm may fail because the firm may not write checks at the required size or may prefer earlier risk profiles.

Partners

Venture capital firms are made up of individual partners. These partners make investment decisions and often take a seat on the board of each portfolio company. This is why fundraising is not only about the firm's brand. It is about the specific person within the firm who will champion the deal.

Partners tend to invest in what they know. A partner with experience in your industry can better understand your value proposition, assess your risks, and identify what makes you different. This relevant experience also gives them confidence that they can help you. Confidence matters because venture capital is relationship driven. A partner must believe not only that the company can succeed, but also that they can contribute meaningfully to that success.

For founders, choosing the right partner is as important as choosing the right firm. The partner becomes a long term collaborator. They may influence hiring decisions, fundraising strategy, partnerships, and major strategic pivots. If the relationship is strong, the partner can be a major advantage. If the relationship is weak, the board dynamic can become stressful and unproductive.

Portfolio

A venture capital firm's portfolio is the collection of companies it has already invested in. Studying a firm's portfolio helps a founder answer several critical questions. Does the firm invest in companies like mine. Does it understand my market. Does it already have competitors or conflicts. Does it have companies that could become partners or customers. Does it have a track record of building winners in this space.

Portfolio company management, being close to the market, sometimes advises the venture firm on whether a new opportunity is worthwhile. This means portfolio fit can influence internal decisions. In addition, if your venture has potential synergies with a portfolio company, that can increase the investor's interest. Synergy can take many forms: shared customers, complementary products, distribution support, technology integration, or joint partnerships.

At the same time, founders must watch for conflicts. If the firm already invested in a direct competitor, it may not invest in you, or it may be restricted by internal policies. Even if no direct competitor exists, the firm may avoid deals that create uncomfortable overlaps. Understanding the portfolio early protects your time and helps you avoid sensitive situations.

Assets

Assets refers to the venture capital firm's ability to provide sufficient capital not only now, but also in future rounds. Most companies seeking venture capital for the first time will require subsequent rounds of capital. Growth consumes cash. Hiring, product development, customer acquisition, and operational scaling all require investment. If an investor cannot participate in follow on rounds, founders may spend significant time constantly searching for new investors, which distracts from building the business.

A venture capital firm with deep resources can support a company across multiple stages. This can stabilize the company's financing, improve investor confidence, and reduce the risk of being underfunded at critical moments. It can also simplify fundraising. When existing investors can lead or anchor follow on rounds, the company often raises capital more efficiently.

However, deep pockets alone are not enough. A founder should also consider how the firm uses its capital. Some firms reserve significant amounts for follow on investments. Others focus on making many new investments and reserve less for later rounds. Understanding this behavior helps founders anticipate whether their investors will be present in the future when the company needs additional funding.

Building a Target List and Approaching Firms Strategically

Once the six variables are clear, the fundraising process becomes more structured. A founder can build a target list of firms that match location, sector, and stage. Then the founder can identify the best partner at each firm, based on experience and interest. After that, the founder can study the portfolio to confirm fit and avoid conflicts. Finally, the founder can evaluate whether the firm has the capacity to support future rounds.

This approach transforms fundraising from a wide, unfocused search into a disciplined campaign. It also improves the quality of conversations. When an investor sees that a founder understands the firm's focus, the conversation becomes more serious. The founder appears prepared and respectful of the investor's strategy, which increases trust.

Consequences of Good Fit and Poor Fit

Finding the right venture capital firm is absolutely critical for companies seeking venture capital. When the fit is right, success typically means more than obtaining money. It means gaining a partner who provides strategic guidance, introductions, credibility, and long term support. It can accelerate growth, improve execution, and reduce mistakes during high pressure scaling phases.

Conversely, failing to find the right firm often leads to raising no capital at all or raising capital from misaligned investors who cannot support the company properly. In the worst cases, founders waste months pitching firms that could never invest, lose time needed to build traction, and face a cash crisis that forces them to shrink plans or shut down. Even if capital is raised, a misaligned investor relationship can create friction in decision making, slow progress, and harm the company's ability to raise future rounds.

For this reason, the first step in raising venture capital is not simply pitching. It is choosing the right audience. A focused approach based on location, sector preference, stage preference, partners, portfolio, and assets gives founders the best chance to raise capital and to build a lasting support system for growth.

OBTAINING VENTURE CAPITAL FOR BUSINESS STARTUP

If you are an inventor or an entrepreneur, obtaining venture capital funding is often one of your biggest concerns, both for your personal goals and for the survival of your business. In the earliest phases, most startups face the same reality: building a product, hiring capable people, testing the market, and reaching customers requires money long before the company can reliably generate it. Even when an entrepreneur has a strong idea, strong energy, and a clear sense of purpose, the company's progress can be limited by cash. This is why venture capital becomes such a common topic in startup life. It is not only about growth, it is often about time, runway, and the ability to keep working until the market responds.

During the dot com boom, venture capitalists were widely perceived as fuel for rapid expansion. Investors financed growth, research, marketing, and ambitious experiments across many new companies, especially in technology and internet related sectors. When that era cooled, many entrepreneurs began to experience a tougher environment. Venture capitalists became more selective, risk tolerance shifted, and funding decisions increasingly depended on measurable traction, credible execution, and realistic business fundamentals. This shift is important for founders to understand because it changes what it means to be fundable. In overheated markets, money can chase stories. In disciplined markets, money chases evidence.

Even in stricter conditions, venture capital does not disappear. It becomes more focused. The standards rise, the process becomes more demanding, and entrepreneurs must present their opportunity with greater clarity. Founders who understand how venture capital works can adapt their approach, target the right investors, and improve their chance of securing funding even when the market is cautious.

Different Forms of Venture Capital Money

Venture capital money can come in different forms, and the source of the capital often shapes expectations, speed, and the kind of support the founder receives.

Some venture capital firms are structured specifically to search for new companies, evaluate them, and invest with the goal of achieving strong long term returns for their investors. These firms receive a very large volume of requests for funding. It is common for a firm to review hundreds or thousands of opportunities over a year and fund only a small number. The selectivity is not necessarily a sign that most businesses are bad. It reflects the venture model itself. Venture funds must invest in companies that can grow large enough to produce meaningful returns relative to the size of the fund. A fund that manages a large amount of capital cannot invest in businesses that are likely to grow slowly or remain small. Therefore, many companies are rejected simply because they do not match the scale requirements of venture capital.

Some venture capital firms also specialize by theme. For example, one firm might focus on technology based startups, while another specializes in real estate development, healthcare, energy, industrial innovation, or consumer products. There are also venture type arrangements used to fund large corporate and infrastructure projects, especially when the project involves significant capital needs and is too risky or complex for traditional financing. In those cases, venture style funding may appear through structured partnerships, staged investment commitments, and performance based milestones.

Understanding these differences helps entrepreneurs avoid confusion. Not every investor who uses the term venture capital behaves like a classic startup venture investor. Some focus on strategic partnerships, some on project finance, and some on technology growth. The founder's job is to identify which category matches their business and their goals.

Angel Investors as an Entry Point

Another way to obtain venture capital for a business startup is through angel investors. An angel investor can be an individual or a group of individuals who invest personal wealth into early stage companies. Angels often enter earlier than venture firms and sometimes invest when the company is still forming, the product is still evolving, or revenue is not yet stable. Because of this, angels can be crucial in helping a startup move from idea to reality.

Angels are sometimes experienced entrepreneurs, executives, or professionals who want to support new ventures and stay connected to innovation. Many provide more than money. They may mentor the founder, offer industry connections, help with recruiting, and provide credibility that makes it easier to attract later investors.

Angels may invest alone or as part of an angel group. An angel group is a network that reviews opportunities together and decides which startups to fund. When a business is selected, the terms are negotiated and the legal paperwork is drafted. Funding may be structured as equity, convertible notes, or other early stage instruments. In some contexts, founders refer to this kind of funding as hard money. However, it is important to be careful with terminology. Hard money often implies lending at high interest with strong collateral requirements, which is more common in real estate than in technology startups. Many angel investments are not loans in the traditional sense. They are structured to convert into equity or to represent ownership directly. The founder should focus less on the label and more on the actual terms, obligations, and control rights.

What angels provide, in addition to funding, is often speed and flexibility. Some angel investors can decide quickly, especially when they know the industry. This can be life saving for startups that need to build momentum and cannot wait through a long institutional investment process.

Media and the Public Image of Venture Funding

In recent years, venture funding has also entered public entertainment through reality television. Some shows focus on inventors who have developed products that could be introduced into the retail market. The format usually involves coaching, presentation, feedback, and competition, with seed money offered to help inventors further develop their product and prepare it for broader distribution. Over several episodes, participants refine their pitch, improve product design, and strengthen the business plan until a final selection is made.

This kind of media presentation can make venture capital appear simple and dramatic: one presentation, one decision, one winner. In reality, venture funding is usually slower and more complex. Investors conduct due diligence, request detailed information, and evaluate the team over time. However, these shows contain a useful lesson: investors are not only evaluating the product. They are evaluating market potential, differentiation, customer demand, and the founder's ability to execute. The winner is often the participant who demonstrates not only a good idea, but also a strong path to commercialization.

For founders, the useful takeaway is that venture funding is partly storytelling and partly proof. You must communicate value clearly, but you must also support your story with evidence that the market wants what you are building.

Why Funding Can Be Harder After Market Booms

After a boom period cools down, funding often becomes harder because investors become more cautious. During boom times, competition among investors can push money toward riskier ideas. Later, when markets slow, investors often shift toward quality, fundamentals, and clear signs of traction. This can be frustrating for founders who feel that they missed a window. But it also creates an advantage for founders who are truly building something strong. In cautious markets, strong companies can stand out more clearly because fewer weak projects are funded.

In tighter periods, investors may ask more detailed questions. They may look for stronger proof of customer demand, clearer unit economics, more disciplined spending, and more credible plans for reaching profitability or sustainable growth. This does not mean venture capital disappears. It means the founder must be more prepared, more precise, and more realistic about risks and execution.

What Increases Your Chances of Getting Venture Capital

If all of this makes you feel concerned or confused, there is good news. Capital still exists. Investors have not stopped investing. They have simply become more selective, and they want stronger reasons to say yes.

Your chances of obtaining venture capital increase when you can present a solid business plan and a credible product concept, supported by evidence. Evidence can take many forms depending on the business. It can be a working prototype, early customer feedback, pilot projects, signed letters of intent, growing user adoption, early revenue, or strong market research that shows a clear demand gap. Investors want to see that the business is not only theoretically attractive but practically achievable.

A strong pitch usually includes several elements.

A clear problem and clear customer. Investors want to know exactly what problem you solve and who experiences that problem. Vague markets and unclear customers weaken investor confidence.

A strong solution that is different. The solution must be meaningfully better than alternatives. Investors look for differentiation that can be defended, whether through technology, brand, distribution, data, partnerships, or execution speed.

A market that is big enough. Venture capital requires scale. Even a great company may not be venture fundable if the market is too small.

A credible team. Investors back people. They want founders who can learn fast, execute, recruit talent, and adapt to change.

A plan for growth and a realistic use of funds. Investors want to know what the capital will achieve, what milestones it will unlock, and how progress will be measured.

A path toward liquidity. Investors need an exit strategy, whether through acquisition or public offering. The founder does not need to predict the exact exit, but should understand how value could be realized.

Preparing for the Process of Approaching Investors

Obtaining venture capital is not only about having a good business. It is also about running a process. Founders who approach fundraising systematically tend to perform better. This includes identifying the right investors, preparing materials, building relationships, and managing timelines.

Founders often start with a short list of investors whose location, sector preference, and stage preference match the company. They then identify specific partners at those firms who are likely to be interested, based on their portfolio history and expertise. They prepare a pitch deck, a summary, and a more detailed plan that can be shared during due diligence. They also ensure that basic company foundations are in place, such as ownership structure, intellectual property clarity, and early financial tracking. These details matter because investors will ask.

Timing also matters. It is easier to raise money when a company has momentum. Momentum can be rapid product progress, customer adoption, or market attention. When founders wait too long and run out of runway, they negotiate from weakness. When founders raise earlier with traction and a clear plan, they negotiate from strength.

A Realistic Conclusion

Venture capitalists may not be throwing money around the way they did in the most overheated periods, but there is still money available for ventures that demonstrate quality, potential, and execution capability. Founders who build real evidence, present a strong plan, and approach the right investors improve their chance of getting funding.

The core message is simple. Venture capital is still accessible, but it rewards preparation. If your product is strong, your market opportunity is real, and your plan is credible, you can still obtain the funding you need to grow your startup and compete at a serious level.

VENTURE CAPITAL FINANCING TIPS

Few words carry more fascination for an entrepreneur than venture capital. The phrase can mean different things to different people, but the emotional meaning is often the same everywhere. It represents the possibility of turning a concept into a real company. For some founders it means transforming an invention from the workbench into a product people can buy. For others it means taking a prototype out of the laboratory and into manufacturing, distribution, and market adoption. Venture capital is often associated with speed, because it can finance rapid development that would otherwise take years. It is also associated with ambition, because it is typically aimed at building companies that can grow quickly and become meaningful players in an industry.

At the same time, venture capital is not free money and it is not suitable for every business. It is a partnership model built around risk and growth. A founder who understands what venture capital is, how it differs from other financing options, and what investors expect is in a much stronger position to raise funds and to use them effectively.

What Venture Capital Really Is

In short, venture capital is money designed for high risk investment in startup enterprises or in companies that are still young but require additional resources to continue expected progress and growth. The investor takes significant risk because early stage companies may fail for many reasons. The product may not work as planned. The market may be smaller than expected. Customers may not adopt quickly. Competitors may react aggressively. The team may struggle to execute. Venture capital exists because some opportunities, despite these risks, can produce extraordinary results if they succeed.

For the investor, venture capital holds out the possibility of large profits in exchange for taking that risk. For the entrepreneur, venture capital offers the chance to build faster and bigger than would be possible with personal savings or slow incremental cash flow. The core trade is ownership for acceleration. The investor provides capital and support. The founder shares a portion of ownership and often shares some decision authority.

How Venture Capital Differs from Bank Financing

Venture capital differs sharply from standard bank financing. A bank loan is a contractual obligation. The borrower must repay principal and interest on a schedule. The bank evaluates risk through collateral, stable cash flow, credit history, and predictable repayment capacity. Most startups cannot meet these requirements, especially at early stages.

Venture capital, by contrast, is usually repaid through ownership value rather than scheduled payments. The investor receives an agreed percentage of the entrepreneur's stock in the business. If the company grows in value, the investor benefits. If the company fails, the investor may lose much or all of the invested capital. This is why venture capital is considered equity oriented financing rather than debt oriented financing.

The investment horizon is also different. Venture capital investors typically expect results over several years, often within three to seven or eight years, depending on the type of company and the stage of investment. A successful outcome may come through an acquisition or through a public listing that allows shares to be sold in public markets. This is why venture capital is deeply connected to the concept of an exit. The investor is not investing to receive interest payments. The investor is investing to eventually convert ownership into a return when liquidity becomes available.

Why IPOs and Acquisitions Matter

In many narratives, the initial public offering is described as the most visible success path. When a company goes public, both investor and entrepreneur can prosper by bringing stock to the public market, because shares become tradeable and valuation may increase. However, not all successful venture backed companies go public. Many achieve strong exits through mergers and acquisitions, where a larger company buys the startup for strategic reasons such as technology, market access, talent, or competitive positioning.

What matters for the founder is understanding that venture capitalists evaluate companies partly through the lens of exit potential. They ask how big the company can become, who might buy it, what conditions would make it attractive, and what timeline seems realistic. A founder does not need to predict the exact acquirer or the exact public market timing, but must demonstrate that there is a plausible route to liquidity if the company executes successfully.

Negotiating Ownership and Terms Before Funding

Usually, the terms of ownership and control are negotiated and agreed before the venture investor concludes financing. This negotiation defines not only the percentage of equity the investor receives, but also governance rights, board structure, protective provisions, and future financing rules. These terms influence how decisions are made during the company's growth, how conflicts are handled, and how value is distributed at exit.

A founder should treat this negotiation as a strategic moment. The easiest time to protect long term outcomes is before money is accepted. After funding, the investor has contractual rights that shape the company's options. This does not mean the founder should distrust investors. It means the founder should understand that venture relationships are built through documented agreements and incentives, and clarity at the beginning reduces problems later.

Common Ways Venture Investments Are Structured

How a venture capitalist chooses to structure an investment depends on the style and track record of the venture fund, as well as the company's stage, risk profile, and bargaining power. Structures can vary widely, but several patterns are common.

Straight equity is a direct purchase of ownership shares. This is common when valuation can be agreed and both sides want a clear ownership relationship.

Equity plus loans or equity like instruments may be used when the investor wants a combination of ownership and additional downside protection. In early stage startups, convertible notes or similar instruments may appear, where investment converts into equity later.

Milestone based structures tie ownership, control, or follow on funding to achievement of certain targets. For example, investor control rights may change as the company meets revenue, product, or market milestones. This approach attempts to align incentives and reduce risk by rewarding execution.

Revenue and sales performance are frequent focal points because they provide measurable signals of market acceptance. Investors often prefer metrics that can be tracked objectively. When there is no stable revenue yet, investors may focus on user growth, retention, pilot success, or other validated indicators.

What Venture Capital Can Do for an Entrepreneur

The advantages of venture capital for an entrepreneur are often clear. The most obvious advantage is the absence of immediate repayment pressure. There is usually no requirement to repay a bank loan because venture capital is typically equity. This can be critical in the first years when a startup must invest heavily and cash is scarce.

Another advantage is risk sharing. The venture capitalist and entrepreneur assume some of the risk together. If the company fails, the investor absorbs losses without demanding repayment in the way a lender would. This reduces the probability that the business collapses under debt obligations before it has a fair chance to prove itself.

There is also a cash flow advantage. Because there are usually no interest payments, funds that would have gone toward debt service can instead be used to hire talent, build the product, acquire customers, and improve operations. For many startups, that difference is the line between stagnation and momentum.

Beyond money, venture capital firms can provide expertise and networks. Knowledgeable and well connected investors can offer introductions to customers, partners, suppliers, and future hires. They can help founders avoid common mistakes in pricing, hiring, product direction, and market strategy. They can also improve credibility. A respected investor can signal quality to the market, making it easier to attract talent, close partnerships, and raise later rounds.

The Main Disadvantage and Why Deals Fail

Sharing ownership and control is often the chief disadvantage of venture capital. By taking venture capital, founders give up a portion of the company and accept external influence in governance. For some entrepreneurs, this is emotionally difficult because the business feels personal. For others, it becomes a practical issue if expectations between founder and investor are misaligned.

This is also a common reason small and inexperienced entrepreneurs fail to close venture deals. Some founders resist the realities of venture capital while still wanting the benefits. Investors will often walk away if they sense that the founder wants capital but refuses accountability, transparency, and shared decision making.

A founder must decide early whether they want a venture path. Venture backed growth typically requires aggressive scaling, frequent measurement, ongoing fundraising, and openness to strategic guidance. If the founder wants full independence, slower growth, and complete control, venture capital may be the wrong tool.

Founder Readiness and What Investors Expect

Before considering venture capital, an entrepreneur should understand the major areas investors evaluate. These are not simple checklist items. They are core indicators of whether the company can become large enough to justify venture investment.

Industry expertise and credibility. Investors want founders who deeply understand their industry, including how customers buy, how competitors compete, and what trends are shaping the market. The founder should show a strong background and awareness of current developments.

Operational and marketing capability. A startup must understand the rigors of running a business, including product development, hiring, budgeting, sales, customer support, and marketing execution. Great technology is not enough if the company cannot sell and deliver reliably.

Third party validation. Investors look for proof that the market needs the product. This can include customer interviews, pilot programs, letters of intent, early revenue, usage data, partnerships, or industry endorsements. External signals reduce uncertainty.

Growth and profitability potential. A venture backed startup must show that it can scale and eventually become profitable. Profitability may not be immediate, but the company should demonstrate that scaling economics can work. This includes pricing power, margins, retention, and customer acquisition dynamics.

These elements matter because venture capital is designed for companies that can become large and valuable relatively quickly compared to traditional small business growth. Investors are looking for evidence that the company can reach meaningful scale.

Fit Between Entrepreneur and Venture Firm

The second major area the entrepreneur must consider is fit with the chosen venture firm. Fit is not only about getting a yes. It is about building a partnership that will last through difficult growth phases.

A founder should understand the venture firm's emphasis. Does it invest in this sector. Does it invest at this stage. Does it prefer certain business models. Does it have a specific view on how companies should scale. What is the expected time frame for holding investments. What is the firm's approach to follow on funding. How involved are the partners.

It is also important to evaluate the venture partners themselves. Investors are individuals. Their style, experience, and communication approach will shape the relationship. A founder should look at the firm's prior investments and outcomes to understand whether the firm has successfully funded and supported similar companies.

Geographic focus also matters because many venture firms prefer to invest close to home where they can be actively involved. A company outside the firm's geography may face less interest or less support after investment.

Choosing a Source of Venture Capital

Choosing a venture capital source is far from simple. The sources of startup capital can range widely. At one end, it might be a wealthy relative or a friend who believes in you and provides seed funding. That kind of capital can be valuable because it can be faster and more flexible. It can help create early progress that later attracts professional investors.

However, personal seed money rarely replaces venture capital at scale. Venture firms exist because many businesses require larger sums, strategic guidance, and staged financing over time. Founders often move through a sequence: personal savings and small seed funding, angel investment, early stage venture capital, and later stage growth capital, depending on the business and the market.

The key is to match the source of funding to the company's needs. If the company needs modest capital and steady growth, venture capital may be unnecessary. If the company requires rapid scaling and significant resources, venture capital may be the most appropriate path.

Final Tips for Founders Seeking Venture Capital

Despite economic slowdowns, there is always money available for entrepreneurs with well thought out novel ideas. What changes in tighter markets is not the existence of capital, but the standards required to access it. Investors demand clearer evidence, stronger preparation, and more disciplined plans.

To improve your chances, focus on research and facts. Know your market size and customers. Know your competitors and why you win. Know your unit economics and growth levers. Build validation through pilots, early sales, user adoption, or credible partnerships. Create a clear narrative supported by data. Approach investors whose sector and stage focus matches your company. Prepare to negotiate terms thoughtfully, with the understanding that venture capital is a partnership that trades ownership for acceleration.

When you treat venture capital as a strategic tool rather than a rescue plan, you increase your probability of securing funding and using it to build a company that can truly scale.

ATTRACTING VENTURE CAPITAL

For a startup business operating in tough economic times, it can be extremely difficult to achieve stability and growth. Costs rise, customers may delay spending, and competition for attention becomes more intense. In this environment, any credible helping hand can make a meaningful difference. Venture capital can be especially valuable because it provides not only funding, but also strategic support, networks, and experienced guidance. For early stage and risk oriented companies, which often have limited operating history and uncertain cash flow, venture capital may be one of the few realistic ways to secure the resources needed to build and scale.

However, venture capital is not easy to obtain. Venture capitalists typically review a large number of opportunities and accept only a very small portion. In many cases, only a small percentage of companies receive an initial interview, and an even smaller percentage receive investment. This selectivity is not meant to discourage entrepreneurs, but it does create a practical truth. If you want venture capital, you must treat fundraising as a serious project that requires preparation, strategy, and persistence.

Understanding the Investor Mindset

To attract venture capital, it helps to understand how investors think. A venture capitalist is not simply asking whether your idea is interesting. They are asking whether your company can become large enough and strong enough to produce a meaningful return. They also evaluate whether your team can handle uncertainty, execute under pressure, and adapt quickly as the market changes. Venture capitalists know that early stage companies often pivot. What they want is a founding team that can learn rapidly, make good decisions, and keep progress moving even when conditions shift.

They also care about credibility and risk management. The irony of venture capital is that it embraces risk, but it does not embrace chaos. Investors accept market and product uncertainty, but they want professionalism in planning, financial reporting, governance, and communication. Many startups fail to get funded not because their product is weak, but because investors sense that the company is poorly organized or that founders cannot present a coherent plan.

Preparation as the Foundation

As with any serious business plan, preparation is vital. Attracting venture capital requires time and manpower. Founders often underestimate how much work fundraising takes. It involves building materials, collecting proof points, refining a narrative, practicing the pitch, reaching out, following up, and managing meetings. If you want an investment firm to take a calculated gamble on you, you must show that you take your own business seriously.

A key part of preparation is having your finances in order. Even at early stage, investors want clean records. They want to see that your spending makes sense, that your numbers match reality, and that you can explain how money is used. If a venture capital firm reviews your books and finds discrepancies, unclear accounting, or missing documentation, you can lose credibility instantly. Investors tend to interpret financial confusion as a warning sign about management quality. You do not need perfect complexity, but you do need clarity, consistency, and transparency.

It also helps to have evidence that other people believe in you. Personal references can strengthen your credibility, especially if they come from respected industry figures, previous employers, customers, partners, mentors, or experienced entrepreneurs. References matter because venture investing is based on trust. Investors are backing a team, and trustworthy signals reduce perceived risk. References can also support your claims about consumer demand for your product, your reliability as a founder, and your ability to execute.

Building a Strong Business Plan and Executive Summary

When seeking financial investment, whether from a bank or an investment firm, having a sound business plan and a clear summary is essential. For venture capital, the executive summary or pitch deck is often the first impression an investor receives. This first impression can strongly affect whether they decide to continue the conversation.

A strong executive summary usually communicates several points quickly. It identifies the problem and why it matters. It explains the solution and why it is different. It describes the customer and the market size. It shows evidence of demand such as early users, pilots, revenue, or partnerships. It introduces the team and why they are suited to win. It outlines the business model and how the company makes money. It includes a clear request, explaining how much funding is needed and how it will be used.

First impressions matter because investors are busy. They must filter quickly. If your materials are unclear, too long, or too vague, the investor may stop reading. Clarity and focus are not cosmetic. They are signals of leadership quality. A founder who communicates clearly is more likely to run the business clearly.

Knowing the Funding Process of Each Investor

It is a good idea to study the funding processes of the firms you plan to approach. Different venture capital firms have different methods. Some have formal application channels. Some prefer warm introductions. Some invest quickly, while others require many internal meetings. Some focus on specific metrics. Some rely heavily on partner judgment. Some require deep technical diligence, especially in specialized sectors.

Research helps you avoid mistakes. It also helps you tailor your approach. If a firm clearly states it focuses on a certain sector or stage, you can adapt your pitch to emphasize the points they care about most. If a firm typically co invests with others, you can anticipate syndication discussions. If a firm prefers local companies, you can highlight your geographic advantage or explain how you will maintain collaboration despite distance.

One of the most effective ways to understand an investor's process is to speak with founders who have already raised money from that firm. These founders can provide insight into what worked and what did not. They can tell you what the partners were sensitive about, how long the process took, what kinds of questions were repeated, and what evidence mattered most. This information is valuable because it comes from direct experience, not marketing language.

Clarity on Use of Capital

Investors want to know where the money will go and why. You should be crystal clear about how capital will be used and how it will help the business succeed. This is not only about listing expenses. It is about showing a plan that connects money to milestones.

A good use of funds explanation includes categories and expected outcomes. For example, a portion may go to product development, with the goal of releasing a market ready version. Another portion may go to hiring, with the goal of building a sales function or strengthening engineering. Another portion may go to marketing and customer acquisition, with the goal of reaching specific user growth or revenue targets. Another portion may go to operations, compliance, or infrastructure, with the goal of supporting scale and reducing risk.

Investors want to see that you are disciplined. They do not want founders who treat funding as a vague safety net. They want founders who treat funding as a tool to achieve specific progress. When you present a clear milestone driven plan, you signal professionalism and increase investor confidence.

Creating a Target List and Running a Process

It is advisable to have at least ten venture capital firms you plan to approach, sometimes more depending on your sector and stage. This is because venture capital is competitive, and rejections are common even for strong companies. Building a list reduces dependence on any single investor and allows you to run fundraising as a process rather than a desperate search.

Each approach should be intentional. Send a tailored letter or message to each firm, showing that you understand their investment focus and why your company fits. Generic messages are often ignored because they signal low effort and poor targeting. A personalized message can highlight the connection between your company and the firm's sector interests, stage focus, and portfolio themes.

After you have sent your initial request, follow up with discipline. If you do not hear back, it may not mean rejection. Investors receive high volumes. A thoughtful follow up after a short period can bring your message back into view. If there is interest, the next step is often a personal meeting where you present the business more fully and answer questions.

Preparing for the Meeting and the Questions

When you move toward a personal meeting, preparation becomes even more important. Investors will test your assumptions. They will ask about your customers, your competition, your pricing, your margins, your sales cycle, your technical advantage, your roadmap, your hiring plan, and your risk factors. They may ask what happens if the market changes or if a competitor copies you. They may challenge your numbers. They may probe your team's weaknesses. These questions are not hostile. They are part of diligence.

You can strengthen your position by anticipating the hardest questions and preparing credible answers. A founder who can explain risks calmly and show mitigation strategies appears more trustworthy. A founder who becomes defensive or vague signals trouble.

Practical Steps That Improve Attractiveness

Several practical actions make a startup more attractive to venture capital.

Demonstrate traction. Even small traction can matter if it shows real demand. This can be revenue, user growth, pilot customers, or strong engagement metrics.

Show proof of market need. Customer interviews, letters of intent, and partnerships can provide third party validation.

Build a strong team story. Investors want to know why you are the right person to build this company, and why your team can execute.

Present a clear narrative. A coherent story that connects problem, solution, market, traction, and plan is often more persuasive than excessive detail.

Maintain clean operations. Basic legal structure, clear ownership, and organized documentation reduce friction in diligence.

FOUR STEPS TOWARDS ATTRACTING VENTURE CAPITAL INVESTMENTS

Most startup companies do not have much capital at the beginning. They often start with a small amount of savings, a modest seed budget, or early revenue that is not yet stable. Because costs arrive immediately while profits arrive later, many startups struggle simply to remain open long enough to reach product market fit and profitability. For this reason, founders often turn to outside investor support to extend their runway and to fund growth until the company can sustain itself.

If you are the owner of a small business, you already know that securing funding can be one of the most difficult business challenges you will face. The difficulty comes from a basic mismatch. Startups need money when they are still uncertain, and most traditional lenders prefer certainty. Venture capital exists specifically to fund uncertainty, but it is selective because the risk is high and only a small portion of companies will generate very large returns.

Why Venture Capital Interest Keeps Growing

Seeking venture capital has become a growing trend due to several factors that make startups more attractive and venture investing more practical. When public markets are healthy and companies can realistically go public, investors gain confidence that successful startups can eventually reach liquidity. This can increase the overall appetite for venture investment. Another factor is the abundance of entrepreneurial talent. More people are building companies, and many have strong skills, global networks, and the ability to move quickly. Promising new technologies also attract investment because they create new markets and reshape old ones. Government policies can also encourage innovation and venture formation through legal frameworks, incentives, research funding, and support for entrepreneurship.

Together, these conditions help explain why venture investors continue to support so many new technologies and business concepts. The venture model relies on the idea that innovation creates outsized winners. When innovation accelerates, the number of potential winners increases, and investors work hard to identify them early.

What Venture Capital Enables You to Do

Venture capital investments provide resources that can help a company grow toward its full potential. Capital can be used in many ways depending on the business model.

You may use funding to hire top talent such as engineers, sales leaders, product designers, and operational managers. You may invest in machinery, production capacity, logistics, or manufacturing improvements if the business involves physical goods. You may need to hire skilled workers and expand labor capacity to deliver services reliably. You may also invest in research and development, testing, and new technology to strengthen your advantage. Many startups use venture capital to accelerate product development, expand market reach, and build the infrastructure needed for scaling.

Venture capital is not only about spending more money. It is about spending the right money at the right time to reach key milestones faster. Investors want to see that capital will translate into measurable progress, not just larger expenses.

To help put you on the track toward securing venture capital, the following four steps explain practical ways to attract the attention of venture capital investors. Each step is important on its own, but the real power comes from combining them into a consistent strategy.

Step One Networking and Building Real Relationships

One of the most important steps is networking. It is often the first gateway to attracting venture capital because venture investing is highly relationship driven. Many investors prefer warm introductions from people they trust, rather than cold emails from strangers. Networking helps your company become visible in the places where investors already spend attention.

Business networking is also an important tool for your company beyond fundraising. It helps you find mentors, partners, customers, suppliers, and future team members. The goal is to place the name of your company in the minds of people in your industry and to create interest around what you are building. Investors often hear about promising startups through repeated exposure. They see the company name in multiple contexts, or they hear about it from several credible sources. This repetition creates a sense that the company is real and moving.

To network effectively, you should be intentional. Attend events where your target investors and industry leaders gather. Participate in startup communities, founder groups, accelerators, and professional associations. When you meet people, focus on genuine connection rather than immediate requests. If you get the chance, collect business cards or contact information, but more importantly, follow up. A network is not a pile of contacts. A network is a set of relationships maintained through communication and mutual value.

Networking also includes building relationships with people who can become advocates. These can be experienced founders, angels, professors, industry executives, or respected professionals. When the time comes to raise money, these advocates can introduce you to investors, validate your credibility, and help you be taken seriously.

Step Two Building an Experienced Team and Proving Execution Capacity

You are going to need a capable team behind you. Investors rarely fund only an idea. They fund a team they believe can execute. One of the first things venture capitalists evaluate is the quality of your organization. They want to see whether the company is structured enough to handle growth. They also look at whether the team is cohesive and committed, because early stage companies face stress and uncertainty. If the team is fragile, execution suffers.

A strong team is usually diverse in skills. It includes product and technical talent, but also includes commercial capability such as marketing, sales, partnerships, and operations. Even early stage startups benefit from clarity about roles, responsibility, and decision making. Investors want to know who builds the product, who sells it, who manages finances, and who leads strategy.

When you build a diverse team of strong minds, you must also learn to communicate the team's credentials. Investors look for evidence that the team has done relevant work before, understands the industry, and can learn quickly. If you have advisors, mentors, or board members with strong reputations, that can also increase investor confidence.

A strong team helps create buzz as well. People talk about companies that have impressive founders and respected talent. That visibility can lead to inbound interest from investors and partners. In venture capital, attention is a form of momentum, and momentum can reduce perceived risk.

Step Three Creating a Professional Presentation That Answers Investor Questions

A professional presentation is essential. Your pitch deck and spoken pitch are not only marketing tools. They are the structure of the investment conversation. A smooth and sophisticated presentation should answer likely questions clearly and should show that you have anticipated risks.

Investors typically want to understand the problem, the solution, the market, competition, traction, business model, team, financial plan, and use of funds. They want to know what makes your company different and why it can win. They want to understand how customers will be acquired and retained. They want to see signs that your company can scale.

A strong presentation also avoids empty optimism. It acknowledges challenges and explains how you will overcome them. This builds trust. Investors become skeptical when founders pretend everything is easy. They prefer founders who understand the difficulties and have credible strategies.

You should practice your presentation repeatedly and refine it based on feedback. Present to mentors, founders, and business associates. Ask what is confusing, what feels weak, what questions remain unanswered. Then update the deck. Continue modifying until the message is clear and the flow is persuasive.

It is also useful to prepare supporting materials. Investors may ask for deeper financial projections, customer references, product demos, pilot results, or market research. Having these ready signals professionalism and speeds up diligence.

Step Four Using Media Coverage to Increase Credibility and Attention

Media coverage brings benefits because it increases visibility and credibility. When your company appears in news outlets, industry publications, podcasts, conferences, or review sites, investors may perceive the company as more real and more validated. Media attention can also attract customers and partners, which improves traction, which then strengthens your investment case.

Anytime you can appear on television, be mentioned in a newspaper, or be featured in an industry platform, it can help. However, the goal is not publicity for its own sake. The goal is credibility and proof of market interest. Investors respond to signals that the market cares.

If your company is in a technology field or connected to the internet economy, you can contact review sites, blogs, and magazines that cover your sector. You can seek interviews, contribute expert commentary, publish thought leadership articles, or demonstrate your product publicly. Writing press releases and submitting them to local newspapers can also catch the eye of potential investors, especially if the story highlights innovation, growth, or unique impact.

To use media effectively, make sure the message is consistent. Your public story should match your investor story. If the media message is vague or exaggerated, it can backfire during due diligence. If the media message is clear and grounded in real progress, it becomes a strong trust signal.

How the Four Steps Work Together

These four steps are strongest when they support each other.

Networking increases your access to investors and creates warm introductions. A strong team makes your story credible and improves execution. A professional presentation turns interest into serious investment conversations. Media coverage amplifies visibility and adds third party validation.

When all four are aligned, the company becomes easier to fund because investor risk perception decreases. They see a company that is known, supported, capable, and progressing. That combination is often what moves a startup from being ignored to being taken seriously.

Final Guidance for Founders

Attracting venture capital is difficult because investors are selective and only a small number of startups receive meetings, and fewer receive funding. But selectivity does not mean the process is random. It means founders must raise their probability of success by building trust signals.

Prepare thoroughly. Keep finances clean. Build relationships in the right circles. Strengthen your team. Communicate clearly. Seek visibility that reflects real progress. If you approach venture capital with discipline and strategy, you increase your chance of moving from an unknown startup to an investable opportunity.

HOW TO RAISE VENTURE CAPITAL

Venture capitalists see thousands, sometimes tens of thousands, of business plans and pitch decks every year. Yet most venture firms fund only a tiny number of companies in that same period. This gap between supply and demand is the first reality every founder must accept. To raise money from a venture capital firm, you must set yourself apart from the crowd. You are not competing only against companies with weak ideas. You are competing against many strong teams, many promising markets, and many well prepared founders.

The reason venture firms invest in so few companies is structural. Venture capital is built on concentration. A firm cannot deeply support hundreds of startups at once, and the returns the firm needs are usually generated by a small number of big winners. This forces investors to be selective and to spend time only on the opportunities that look capable of becoming large, durable businesses. As a founder, your job is to show that your company is not merely a product, not merely a feature, and not merely a nice small business. You must show that it is a venture fundable company, meaning it has the potential to scale significantly and to produce a meaningful return.

Why Every Venture Capitalist Is Different

Every venture capitalist is different. From the outside, venture investors can look similar because they all speak the language of innovation, growth, and disruption. But their expectations, strategies, and internal rules are often very different. Some firms are comfortable investing very early when uncertainty is high. Others only invest when traction is proven. Some focus on a small number of sectors. Others invest across many categories. Some are very hands on with portfolio companies. Others prefer a lighter involvement style.

Understanding these differences is not an optional detail. It determines whether you are pitching the right person and whether you are framing your company in a way that matches what they want. A founder who treats all investors the same wastes time. A founder who learns how specific investors think gains speed and credibility.

Two Common Investor Styles Herd Investors and Contrarian Investors

Some venture capitalists like to follow the herd. This means they invest in categories where many other investors are also placing bets. They may prefer hot markets because they believe that when a space is hot, it attracts talent, customers, partnerships, and attention. Those ingredients can accelerate growth. In a hot market, you may raise money more easily if your company is strong and your team looks capable, because investors want exposure to the trend.

For example, if online communities, artificial intelligence, or a certain consumer trend is attracting large investment, a company in that space may receive more investor interest simply because the category is popular. This does not mean the company will succeed automatically. It means the door to funding can open faster because investors are actively searching for opportunities in that space.

Other venture investors take a contrarian approach. They prefer to fund against the grain. They look for value where others are not paying attention. They may invest in enterprise software when consumer apps are dominating headlines. They may fund a company that many other investors have passed on, not because they enjoy disagreement, but because they believe the market is mispricing the opportunity. Contrarian investors often feel that the best returns come from being early and different, not from competing in crowded trends.

For a founder, the key is to identify which type of investor you are talking to and tailor your pitch accordingly. A herd investor may respond strongly to momentum, market expansion, and category excitement. A contrarian investor may respond strongly to overlooked customer needs, unfair advantages, and clear reasons why the market is wrong.

Why Many Firms Avoid Duplicate Investments in the Same Subcategory

Venture investors typically do not make multiple investments in the same subcategory. This is not always true, but it is common. Within a broad category like internet startups, a firm may invest in a company in the online shopping subcategory. If you are also an online shopping company, it is unlikely that the same firm will invest in you. The reason is conflict and focus. Investors do not want to fund two companies that compete directly because it creates conflict in board discussions, strategy conversations, and access to sensitive information. It also forces the investor to choose sides, which is risky and uncomfortable.

Because of this, it is often unwise to pitch a firm that already invested in a close competitor. Even if your company is stronger, the firm may be structurally unable to invest. The better strategy is to research a firm's portfolio first. If a direct overlap exists, move on and focus your energy on a firm that has no conflict and is still looking for a winner in your category.

Why Venture Funds Need Big Outcomes

Because venture investors make relatively few investments over the course of their careers, they have to select companies they believe can become big. Not every firm invests only in huge outcomes. Some diversify by investing in a mix of high risk large upside opportunities and smaller lower risk companies. But in general, most venture investments must be aimed at large companies to deliver the returns that the investors in the fund expect.

This is where many founders misunderstand what they are selling. Many pitches present features or products, but not venture fundable companies. A feature can be useful but it may not build a large business. A product may solve a problem but may not scale. Venture capitalists are looking for companies that can grow to meaningful scale, capture a large market, and defend their position. This is why a founder must explain not only what the product does, but also why the company can become large, why customers will keep buying, and why competitors cannot easily take the market away.

The Reality of Funding Challenges

Many people believe they have the next multi million dollar idea that will revolutionize an industry. That confidence is valuable, but funding is often the greatest obstacle to moving from idea to reality. Raising capital is difficult in any economy and even harder when the economy is struggling. Elevator speeches and fancy poster boards might get you to the front door of an office if you are lucky, but venture capital requires more than a clever introduction. It requires proof, clarity, and credibility.

The objective of any venture capital firm is to financially benefit its investors through your company. The firm will invest, help guide the company, and seek an exit strategy. They are not funding you as a personal favor. They are buying into an opportunity. That is why preparation is critical. Founders must understand that venture capital is a structured relationship with expectations, timelines, reporting, and governance.

Five Guidelines for Funding Through Venture Capitalists

Guideline One Launch Progress Matters More Than the Idea
Most venture capitalists are not looking to buy an idea. They want to see how well you have launched your company so far. They want proof that you can execute. If they see that you have not put forth effort to build the company, they will not put forth effort to fund it. Investors want to back founders who take initiative, move fast, and create momentum with limited resources.

This does not mean you need a fully mature company. You may still be early. But you should be able to demonstrate progress. Progress can include a prototype, a working product, early users, pilot customers, signed letters of intent, revenue, partnerships, or clear market validation. Even small traction shows that the idea is grounded in reality.

The text suggests that long business plans are not helpful. While the wording is exaggerated, the point is true in spirit. Investors rarely fund because you wrote a long document. They fund because you show a clear opportunity supported by evidence. Your written materials should be concise and strong. Instead of producing a massive plan, focus on building a strong pitch deck, a clear narrative, and measurable results. Then explain the direction you see the company going and ask for funding to accelerate that direction.

Guideline Two Know the Investors and Choose the Right Type

In today's market, most venture capitalists operate through structured firms. This can make the process feel less personal than founders expect. But relationships still matter. You must understand who you are speaking to and what type of investor you need.

Different investors focus on different stages. Some invest in the startup phase, others in the expansion phase, and others in later phases such as buyouts or recapitalizations. If you pitch a later stage investor with an early stage startup, you will likely be rejected. Not because your company is weak, but because the investor's mandate is different.

Do your research before any meeting. Study the investor's website, portfolio, and investment themes. Identify whether they have funded companies similar to yours. Look for patterns in check size, stage, geography, and sector. If possible, speak with founders who have raised money from that investor. Ask what the process was like, what questions mattered, and how supportive the investor has been after investing.

Trust is central. It is hard for anyone to give money to someone they do not know or trust. The easiest way to build trust is to show competence, transparency, and preparation. Also, when you meet an investor, listen carefully. Investors often share insights that can strengthen your business. They invest because they believe the company can grow, and their experience can be as valuable as their money.

Guideline Three Back to the Basics Keep the Pitch Clear and Tangible

Once you have started your company and identified the right investor type, it is time to prepare your presentation. Keep your pitch simple enough that anyone can understand the business model quickly. Clarity is power. If you cannot explain your business simply, investors assume you do not understand it deeply enough.

Present with confidence, but avoid arrogance. Dress professionally, speak clearly, and show that you have direction. Investors evaluate not only your idea but also your leadership presence. They want to know whether you can recruit talent, sell customers, and handle pressure.

Bring tangible evidence. If you have a product, show it. If you have a prototype, bring it or demonstrate it. If you have customer feedback, share it. Investors respond strongly to things they can see and touch, because tangible proof reduces uncertainty.

During the pitch, pause and ask whether the investor understands. Invite questions. If you do not know an answer, say so. A thoughtful investor may even help you find the answer, and honesty builds credibility. Finally, be clear about how much funding you are asking for and what stake the investor will receive. Investors dislike vague requests. They want precise terms and a clear plan for how the capital will be used.

Guideline Four Do Not Depend on One Investor Create Options

Do not put all your eggs in one basket. If a venture capitalist likes your business model, they may negotiate aggressively on terms. You should be prepared with a written proposal and a clear set of documents. Include information about your company structure, bylaws, ownership, current financials, and operating agreements. This helps negotiations and signals professionalism.

Approaching multiple investors creates options. When more than one investor is interested, it creates competition and increases your credibility. Investors notice when others are paying attention. Competitive interest can lead to better terms, lower dilution, and more founder friendly structures. It can also help you select the best partner, not just the first one who says yes.

This does not mean you should play games. Investors can detect manipulation. The goal is simply to run a real process so you have alternatives. When you have alternatives, you negotiate from strength.

Guideline Five Maintain the Relationship After Funding

Once your company is funded, maintaining a relationship with investors is essential. Venture capital is not a one time transaction. It is an ongoing partnership. Investors may not manage daily operations, but they can influence major decisions and future funding. They also have the ability to stop participating in follow on rounds, which can affect your company's runway.

Maintain consistent communication. Provide regular updates. Share financial reports and key metrics. Explain what is working, what is not, and what you are doing about it. Investors prefer transparency over surprises. When founders hide problems, trust breaks. When founders communicate problems early, investors can help solve them.

Healthy relationships between companies and investors can lead to future expansion. If you perform well and communicate well, investors may support additional rounds, introduce you to strategic partners, help with recruiting, and strengthen your path to exit opportunities.

Final Perspective

Because bank funding can be difficult to obtain in many economic conditions, many entrepreneurs turn to venture capitalists. But venture capital requires preparation. Know exactly how much money you need and why. Know how much of the company you are willing to give up. Approach the right investors based on stage and sector. Create multiple options so you can negotiate fairly. Then, once funded, maintain strong communication and a professional relationship.

If you follow these guidelines, using venture capital to fund your ideas becomes much smoother. You increase your chance not only of raising money, but of raising it from investors who can truly help you build a successful company.

ELEMENTS OF A TERM-SHEET

If you have successfully sold your business concept to a venture capitalist, the next step is usually the term sheet. A term sheet is essentially an offer letter that outlines how much the investor will invest, at what price, and under what terms. It is not always the final legal agreement, but it sets the direction for everything that follows. Once you sign a term sheet, the lawyers will convert it into long, binding contracts. That is why understanding the term sheet matters so much. It defines the economic deal, meaning who gets what, and it defines the control deal, meaning who can decide what.

Term sheets can be incredibly simple, sometimes only one or two pages, or they can be complex and lengthy. Complexity is not automatically bad, but it is often a warning sign. If you receive an extremely complex and lengthy term sheet early, you should think carefully about whether that investor will be easy to work with. If the first document you receive is overloaded with legal detail and investor protections, the final investor rights and subscription agreements are likely to be even more complex. That complexity usually means more legal work, more negotiation, more time, and higher legal bills. In many venture deals, the company ends up paying the legal costs, so complexity can become a direct cost for you.

The term sheet is also the place where founders often make avoidable mistakes. Many founders focus almost entirely on valuation because valuation feels like the headline number. But control and protection provisions often matter more. A slightly higher valuation can be erased by harsh liquidation preferences, aggressive anti dilution provisions, or heavy protective rights that limit your freedom. A strong founder negotiates the whole package, not only the price.

Basics of the Offer

This section explains the main economic outline of the deal. Even if you do not understand every legal term, these items should be clear and specific.

Closing date

The closing date is an estimated date when the legal work is expected to be completed and when you will receive the money. This date is important because startups operate on runway. A deal that closes later than expected can create cash pressure. It is wise to build a buffer because legal work and due diligence often take longer than founders hope. The closing date is not always guaranteed, but it sets expectations about timing.

Investors

This describes who is participating in the round. You may have more than one venture capital firm investing, especially in later rounds, and you may also have angels or strategic investors joining. The investor group matters because different investors bring different expectations, styles, and networks. It also matters because syndication can affect control. If several investors join, board seats and voting rights may be shared or negotiated differently.

Amount raised

This states how much money the investor is providing. It should be defined clearly, because it influences dilution, runway, and the future financing plan. The amount raised should also make sense relative to your milestones. Investors will ask what you can achieve with that amount. If the amount is too small, you may need to raise again too quickly. If it is too large, you may give away more ownership than necessary at an early stage.

Price per share

This is what the investor will pay per share. It is directly linked to valuation, but it also depends on the capital structure. Many founders look only at the price and forget to examine how many shares exist and what types of shares are being issued.

Pre money valuation

The pre money valuation is what the investor believes your company is worth before their money is added. This number drives dilution. The higher the valuation, the less equity you give up for the same investment amount. However, a higher valuation can create pressure in the next round because future investors will expect meaningful growth. A valuation that is too high too early can lead to down rounds later, which can trigger painful anti dilution clauses.

Capitalization

Capitalization describes the share structure. It usually includes pre and post investment share counts. It states how many shares are outstanding before the investment and how many will be outstanding after the investment. This matters because dilution is determined by the total share count, not only by valuation. Capitalization tables also reveal whether option pools are included and whether they are created before or after the investment, which can change how dilution is allocated.

Basics of the Terms

After the offer basics, the term sheet usually moves into the rights and protections that come with the investor's shares. These terms often determine whether you keep operational control and how value is distributed at exit.

Dividends and the type of preferred stock

Venture investors usually buy preferred stock, not common stock. Preferred stock can come with dividend rights. Sometimes dividends are non cumulative, meaning they do not accumulate if unpaid. Sometimes they are cumulative, meaning unpaid dividends stack up over time and must be paid later, often at liquidation or redemption. Cumulative dividends can be a hidden cost. They can make the investment look founder friendly on valuation while shifting more value to investors later without additional cash invested.

Some preferred stock is participating preferred. This structure can allow the investor to receive their money back first and then still participate in the remaining proceeds as if they were common shareholders. This can reduce founder returns significantly at modest exit values.

Because dividends and preferred structures vary, this section is a major negotiation point. Founders often try to avoid cumulative dividends and to limit participation features, especially if they reduce the fairness of outcomes.

Liquidation preference

Liquidation preference defines what happens when the company is sold, liquidated, or goes public. Many founders assume that ownership percentage determines the exit split. For example, if an investor owns 40 percent, they expect the investor to get 40 percent. Liquidation preference changes that. It establishes a priority payout for preferred investors before common shareholders receive proceeds.

Straight preferred typically means the investor gets their investment back before common receives anything, but then the investor must choose either to take that preference or convert into common and share proportionally. Participating preferred allows the investor to take the preference and then still share the remainder. This is why it is often called getting paid twice.

Liquidation preference is one of the most powerful terms in the term sheet because it directly affects founder outcomes. It also affects employee outcomes because employee options usually convert into common.

Liquidation preference example and why it matters

In a simple scenario, an investor puts five million into a company valued at five million pre investment and gets half the company. With straight preferred, if the company sells for seven million, the investor gets their five million back first and the founders split the remaining two million. If the company sells for ten million, the investor might convert to common and split the ten million evenly, giving both sides five million.

Under this structure, the investor only begins to earn meaningful profit at higher exit values. During boom markets, investors sometimes accepted this because expectations were high.

Participating preferred changed the dynamic. In the same example, if the company sells for seven million, the investor gets five million first, then the remaining two million is split by ownership, giving the founders only one million. If the company sells for ten million, the investor gets five million first, then splits the remaining five million, giving founders two and a half million. This means the investor earns returns at lower exit values, while founders need a much higher sale price to achieve the same payout.

Some term sheets also include a multiple, such as one and a half times. That means the investor gets one and a half times their investment back before any split occurs. This can create a high hurdle for founders, especially if the company is sold at a moderate valuation.

Voting rights

Voting rights describe how the investor can vote their shares. Investors often require protective voting provisions that give them power over key decisions even if they do not own a majority of shares. This may include requiring investor approval for major actions such as selling the company, issuing new shares, changing the charter, borrowing significant money, or changing board composition.

Protective provisions

Protective provisions are designed to protect the investor's downside. They give the investor veto rights over major corporate actions. Investors will want the ability to block decisions that could harm their position. Founders should ensure these rights are reasonable. The challenge is to balance protection with flexibility. If protective provisions are too broad, the company can become difficult to run because too many decisions require approval.

Anti dilution provisions

Anti dilution provisions protect investors if the company raises a later round at a lower valuation. Without anti dilution, all shareholders dilute proportionally. With anti dilution, earlier investors can receive adjustments that preserve their ownership percentage or reduce the impact of dilution, often at the expense of founders and employees.

The example given shows how painful this can be. If a new investor enters at a lower valuation, the earlier investor's percentage may be protected while the founder's share shrinks dramatically. There are different types of anti dilution, such as full ratchet and weighted average. Full ratchet is harsher. Weighted average is more common and typically less extreme. This section is critical because it determines who pays the price when fundraising conditions worsen.

Redemption rights

Redemption rights describe what happens if the company does not grow fast enough to reach an acquisition or IPO but continues operating. Investors may eventually want their money back. Redemption rights allow them to demand repayment of their investment, sometimes with accrued dividends, after a certain number of years, often beginning around year five and paid over time.

These rights can create pressure on a company that becomes stable but not high growth. From an investor perspective, redemption prevents capital from being stuck forever. From a founder perspective, redemption can be dangerous because it can force a company into a sale or financial restructuring simply to satisfy the investor's demand.

Representations and warranties

Representations and warranties are promises you make about the company. They cover things like financial statements, customer contracts, intellectual property ownership, litigation status, compliance, and other factual claims. They matter because if something is false, the investor can back out or seek remedies. This section becomes the backbone of due diligence. After signing the term sheet, investors will review your books and records carefully. If they find issues that contradict your claims, they may renegotiate or walk away.

Conditions to closing

Conditions to closing are requirements that must be satisfied before the investment is finalized. These can include completion of due diligence, legal filings, board approvals, and other procedural steps. This is another escape route for the investor. It is normal to have conditions, but founders should be aware that vague or broad conditions can allow the investor to delay or withdraw if they change their mind.

Additional Terms in More Extensive Term Sheets

The items above cover the basics, but longer term sheets often include additional investor rights. These rights are usually designed to protect the investor's position and increase the probability of a good exit.

Information rights

Investors may require regular financial reporting, budgets, and updates. This allows them to monitor performance and intervene if necessary.

Participation rights in future rounds

Investors often want the right to invest in future rounds to maintain their ownership percentage. This is called pro rata participation. It can be reasonable, but founders should understand how it affects future fundraising dynamics.

Registration rights

If the company goes public, investors may demand that the company covers the cost of registering shares for sale. This can create administrative costs for the company.

Investor approval requirements

Certain actions may require investor approval, such as issuing new securities, making acquisitions, selling major assets, or changing executive compensation plans. Again, the balance is between protection and operational flexibility.

Non disclosure and non compete provisions

Some term sheets include confidentiality provisions and limitations on competitive behavior. These must be examined carefully, especially because overly broad non compete provisions can restrict founder freedom.

Expiration date and no shop provision

Term sheets often include an expiration date, meaning the offer is only valid for a limited time. This pushes the founder to respond quickly. Term sheets may also include a no shop provision, which prevents you from seeking other offers for a period of time. Investors use no shop provisions to stop founders from using the term sheet as leverage to get better terms elsewhere.

From a founder's perspective, the goal is to have multiple term sheets at the same time. Competing offers give you negotiation power. If you sign a no shop too early, you lose leverage. That is why founders often try to delay agreeing to a strict no shop until they have explored alternatives.

Negotiation Priorities Valuation Versus Control

Your job is to negotiate the deal to your best advantage. Many founders focus too much on valuation because it is the easiest number to compare. But you should pay close attention to control provisions and economic protections. Liquidation preferences, participating preferred, anti dilution clauses, protective provisions, and redemption rights can reshape the entire outcome of the deal.

A slightly lower valuation with clean terms can be far better than a higher valuation with harsh preferences and heavy control rights. Term sheets are about the full package. If you negotiate thoughtfully and understand how each term affects both control and exit outcomes, you can protect your ability to build the company while still giving investors a fair return opportunity.

MAIN REASONS COMPANIES ARE REJECTED BY VENTURE CAPITAL FUNDS

Do not be frustrated if you have failed to raise capital from venture capital funds. Only a very small percentage of companies raise capital from venture capital funds, and in difficult market environments that percentage becomes even smaller. Rejection is often not a sign that your idea is worthless. It is usually a sign that your company does not match what that specific fund is designed to invest in, or that your timing is not aligned with the investor's current priorities.

Venture capital is built on selection. A fund might review hundreds or thousands of opportunities to invest in only a handful. That means many good businesses will be rejected simply because the fund has limited capacity, limited capital per year, and a strict internal focus. If you understand the most common reasons for rejection, you can improve your approach, target the right investors, and reduce wasted effort.

Deal size is too small

One of the most common reasons is that the deal is too small. Many venture capital funds have mandates that set minimum investment sizes. Some funds cannot write checks smaller than one million, while others may require ten million or more, depending on their strategy and fund size. This is not arrogance. It is math. A large fund must deploy a large amount of capital and cannot spend time on small deals that will not move the needle for their return targets.

If you are seeking a small amount of capital, some venture funds will not even take the meeting because the investment would not fit their structure. In this case, the problem is not your company. The problem is the mismatch between your funding need and their investment model. The solution is to target investors whose typical check size matches what you are raising, such as angels, micro venture funds, seed funds, accelerators, or strategic partners who invest smaller amounts.

New company with very early stage risk

Many venture funds avoid extremely early stage startups, especially those that are only an idea without product, traction, or validation. While some venture investors specialize in seed deals, many prefer to see evidence that the company has moved beyond concept stage.

If you are a startup at the earliest stage, you may have better results with alternatives. These can include startup funding programs, angel investors, incubators, accelerators, government grants, research funding, or competitions. These sources are often designed to support early experimentation and product development. Venture funds tend to prefer companies that have already proven something meaningful, such as early product adoption, strong engagement, pilot customers, or early revenue.

Lack of existing revenue or lack of traction proof

A lack of revenue is a frequent reason for rejection, especially when the investor prefers companies with proven market demand. Consider the investor's point of view. If they compare two companies, one with no revenue and one with three years of revenue, the second company appears less risky. Even if the first company has huge potential, investors must justify risk to their partners and their fund.

This does not mean you must be profitable to raise venture capital. Many venture backed companies raise money before profitability. But you usually need proof of demand. If you do not have revenue, you need other signals such as user growth, retention, engagement, pilots, signed contracts, letters of intent, partnerships, or clear evidence that customers want what you are building.

If you have made a profit, even a small profit, show it. Profit signals discipline, pricing power, and operational competence. Many people say it is far harder to raise capital without revenue. Whether the multiple is exactly ten times is less important than the practical reality. Without revenue, your story must do more work. You must compensate with stronger evidence, clearer market logic, and stronger traction indicators.

Too technical and difficult to understand

Sometimes founders have strong ideas but cannot explain them clearly in plain language. Venture investors may be smart, but they are not specialists in every niche. If they cannot quickly understand what you do, why it matters, and why customers will pay, they will reject the deal.

A famous principle often repeated in investing is that people avoid investing in what they do not understand. The practical meaning is simple. If your pitch is overly technical, full of jargon, or unclear about the business value, investors will hesitate. They may fear hidden risks. They may worry that customer adoption will be difficult. They may assume the market is too small or too complex.

The solution is not to remove technical depth. The solution is to translate it into outcomes. Explain what problem you solve, for whom, and what measurable improvement you deliver. Then show how your technology creates that advantage. A good pitch can be understood at two levels. A simple level for the core concept and a deeper level for technical diligence.

Relying too much on corporate advisors and brokers

Advisors and brokers can help, but they cannot replace founder involvement. If you do nothing and rely entirely on corporate advisors, raising capital becomes extremely difficult. Investors want to see the founder's commitment, clarity, and ability to sell. Fundraising is not something you outsource fully. You can get support in structuring, introductions, and documentation, but you must lead the process.

You also must improve the business while fundraising. Investors look for progress. That progress can include product development, customer acquisition, partnerships, and market validation. Advisors cannot build your product or create your traction. They can help you communicate it, but they cannot create it for you.

A founder who works closely with advisors, uses them strategically, and remains fully involved sends a strong signal. A founder who hides behind advisors sends the opposite signal. Investors may interpret it as lack of leadership or lack of confidence.

Failing to show that you do not need the money to survive

There is an ironic truth in venture capital. Investors often prefer to invest in businesses that are already sustainable or already on track. They want companies that do not need capital to survive, but need capital to grow. This is because survival funding is risky. If a company is raising money to avoid collapse, investors worry that the money will disappear into basic expenses without creating real growth.

A company that can demonstrate stability has bargaining power. Even if growth is still early, showing that you have a functioning engine changes how investors see you. You are not asking them to rescue you. You are asking them to accelerate you. This shift changes the negotiation dynamics and increases investor interest.

You can demonstrate this by showing strong unit economics, customer retention, recurring revenue, efficient customer acquisition, or a clear path to break even. Even if you are not fully profitable, showing that the business could survive through disciplined execution makes you more attractive.

The Core Principle Build First, Then Raise

Rule number one is to build up your business first, make it worthwhile, then talk to venture capital funds. The goal is not to raise capital first and then build the business. While there are exceptions, most successful venture backed companies show evidence that the business is real before major venture funding arrives.

This evidence can take different forms depending on the type of business. For consumer platforms, it can be the number of users, user growth rate, retention, engagement, and network effects. For enterprise software, it can be pilots, paid contracts, a clear sales pipeline, and strong customer satisfaction. For hardware, it can be prototypes, manufacturing readiness, and demand validation through preorders or partnerships.

Even the most state of the art ideas require validation. There is no shortage of great concepts, but investors want proof that the market responds.

Assets Are Not Only Financial

When discussing company assets, it is not only about financial statements. Sometimes the strongest asset is a network, a user base, or a proprietary distribution channel. User numbers, growth rate, and engagement can be treated as assets because they can be converted into revenue through smart business models.

A classic example often discussed in the tech world is Hotmail being acquired because it had millions of registered users. The acquiring company could use that user base for marketing and expansion. The lesson is that your value may not only be current revenue. It may be what your company can realistically bring to the market, the leverage you have built, and the unique advantage you can scale.

How to Use Rejection Constructively

If you are rejected, treat it as data. Identify which reason applies.

If the deal is too small, change your target investor list.
If you are too early, focus on traction and early proof.
If you lack revenue, build stronger validation metrics.
If you are too technical, simplify your story and lead with outcomes.
If you relied too much on advisors, become the driver of the process.
If you look desperate for survival, build stability and show growth use of funds.

Rejection is not the end. It is feedback. When you address the underlying reason and return with stronger evidence, you often become investable to a new set of investors.

DISCLAIMER

Introduction

By using this book, you accept this disclaimer in full.

No advice

The book contains information. The information is not advice, and should not be treated as such.

If you think you may be suffering from any medical condition you should seek immediate medical attention. You should never delay seeking medical advice, disregard medical advice, or discontinue medical treatment because of information in the book.

No representations or warranties

To the maximum extent permitted by applicable law and subject to section below, we exclude all representations, warranties, undertakings and guarantees relating to the book.

Without prejudice to the generality of the foregoing paragraph, we do not represent, warrant, undertake or guarantee:

- that the information in the book is correct, accurate, complete or non-misleading;
- that the use of the guidance in the book will lead to any particular outcome or result.

Limitations and exclusions of liability

The limitations and exclusions of liability set out in this section and elsewhere in this disclaimer: are subject to section 6 below; and govern all liabilities arising under the disclaimer or in relation to the book, including liabilities arising in contract, in tort (including negligence) and for breach of statutory duty.

We will not be liable to you in respect of any losses arising out of any event or events beyond our reasonable control.

We will not be liable to you in respect of any business losses, including without limitation loss of or damage to profits, income, revenue, use, production, anticipated savings, business, contracts, commercial opportunities or goodwill.

We will not be liable to you in respect of any loss or corruption of any data, database or software.

We will not be liable to you in respect of any special, indirect or consequential loss or damage.

Exceptions

Nothing in this disclaimer shall: limit or exclude our liability for death or personal injury resulting from negligence; limit or exclude our liability for fraud or fraudulent misrepresentation; limit any of our liabilities in any way that is not permitted under applicable law; or exclude any of our liabilities that may not be excluded under applicable law.

Severability

If a section of this disclaimer is determined by any court or other competent authority to be unlawful and/or unenforceable, the other sections of this disclaimer continue in effect.

If any unlawful and/or unenforceable section would be lawful or enforceable if part of it were deleted, that part will be deemed to be deleted, and the rest of the section will continue in effect.

Law and jurisdiction

This disclaimer will be governed by and construed in accordance with Swiss law, and any disputes relating to this disclaimer will be subject to the exclusive jurisdiction of the courts of Switzerland.

CONCLUSION

If you are an inventor or an entrepreneur with your eyes set on development or starting a business, then funding is a prime concern of yours. All the ideas in the world will not bring a pay check to your bank if you do not have the capital to evolve those ideas into a solid, workable business. The phrase, "You have to spend money to make money" is incredibly true, at least when it comes to start ups and creating the business of your dreams.

Luckily, the funding you need is available through venture capital. You may have heard of it, but you may not know exactly what it is, or if such a thing can help you. This guide explores almost every avenue of venture capital investing; what it is, who are venture capitalists, how to qualify for it, how to interest a venture capital firm and much, much more.

The capital you need is out there, IF you know how to get it, and this book can help you do that. It truly is everything the Entrepreneur needs to know about Venture Capital and Start-up Fundraising.

www.ingramcontent.com/pod-product-compliance
Lightning Source LLC
LaVergne TN
LVHW022313200926
848481LV00004B/1330